THE WORLD'S YOUNGEST GENERAL

Dr. Kuhoi Zhimomi & Khekaho Zhimomi

THE WORLD'S YOUNGEST GENERAL

General Kaito Sukhai
22 May 1933 - 4 August 1968

"An army of sheep led by a lion is better than an army of lions led by a sheep."

Alexander the Great

Dedication

This book is dedicated to the thousands of brave Naga fighters who died for the cause of Naga freedom.

THE WORLD'S YOUNGEST GENERAL

Copyright © 2022 by Dr. Kuhoi Zhimomi & Khekaho Zhimomi

ISBN: 978-1-8384838-7-6

All rights reserved.
No part of this publication may be reproduced, stored in a retrieval system, or transmitted in any form or by any means, electronic, mechanical, photocopying or otherwise, without prior written consent of the publisher except as provided for under United Kingdom copyright law. Short extracts may be used for review purposes with credits given.

Scriptures taken from the Holy Bible, New International Version®, NIV®. Copyright © 1973, 1978, 1984, 2011 by Biblica, Inc.™ Used by permission of Zondervan. All rights reserved worldwide. www.zondervan.com The "NIV" and "New International Version" are trademarks registered in the United States Patent and Trademark Office by Biblica, Inc.™

Published by
Maurice Wylie Media
Your Inspirational Book Publisher

Based in Northern Ireland and distributing across the world.

For more information visit
www.MauriceWylieMedia.com

Statement from the Authors

No part of the contents of this book was fabricated or overstated. It is a thoughtful narration by first-hand living witnesses which utilises documented evidence based on the life of a young leader who gave his life for the cause of Naga freedom.

Contents

	Tributes	13
	Introduction	15
One	The Birth of a Legend	19
Two	The Initial Years	35
Three	The First Indo-Naga Battle	48
Four	The Bracing of Naga Armed Forces	60
Five	The Cost of Freedom	69
Six	His inspiration to Nationalism and the Era of his Fighters	80
Seven	The First Mission to East Pakistan	108
Eight	The London Escapade	132
Nine	Homeland, here we come!	146
Ten	The Twists and Turns of Past Policies	152
Eleven	The Smothered Star	186
	Epilogue	200
Appendix	Primary Sources of Information	206
	Book References	207

Tributes

"He was 'the world's Youngest General,' 'the Born General,' and also a 'statesman.'"
British Broadcasting Corporation (BBC)

"General Kaito saved my tribes from the annihilation of Indian army I will be forever indebted to him. I have been involved for 65 years in the Naga National Movement, and I had never seen or known anyone who was more audacious, of greater genius or more committed than Kaito. People go through pains and turmoil but what Kaito went through was unrivaled"
Hopong P. Yimchunger first President of Yimchunger (Yimkhiung) Tribal Council and former Angh (Governor) FGN.

"Kaito had no dread, no worries or loss of composure; he was a self-assured person. He was not just a great military General, but a visionary politician, and a clever diplomat. He was one of a kind."
Dr. H.S. Rotokha, former President Sümi Tribal Council and Executive member FGN.

"Kaito was a born General, a clever diplomat, an insightful politician; to be specific, he was everything."
Dr. Huskha Yepthomi, former Personal Security Officer to General Kaito and former President Sümi Hoho.

"Indeed, late General Kaito made a niche in the history of Naga National Movement"
Z. Lohe, former Speaker Nagaland Legislative Assembly.

"Kaito was a two-edged sword: intelligent, agile and brave" **Zhevishe Aye,** former Lt. Colonel Naga Army.

"In Heaven there is Almighty God, on earth Kaito was my god"
Kiyeshe Zhimomi, former Naga Army.

"He was strong, both physically and mentally. He was a man of vision who loved his soldiers from his heart."
Tokhuvi Tuccu (Muru), former Brigadier Naga Army.

"A man like General Kaito has not yet been born among the Nagas."
Vikuho Zhimomi, former Personal Security Officer to General Kaito and first batch Naga army.

"He was a legend, we grew up hearing many great things about him. He is an inspiration for the generations and will be forever remembered as a hero to Nagas in general and Sümis in particular."
H. Khekuto Khulu IAS, (Rtd) first IAS among the Sümi tribesman.

"Kaito's courage was unexplainable. He was an ever-growing legend."
Nirmal Nibedon, Author of *The Night of the Guerrillas*.

Introduction

During the Second World War, the British Allied forces had set a camp somewhere in the eastern frontiers of the Himalayas, at a tiny Naga village called Ghukhuyi. A young boy would hang around with those allied soldiers, at every given chance, so that he could familiarise himself with their conduct which was his passion. After a few encounters with this young boy, the allied personnel remarked that the boy would one day grow up to be an excellent soldier, but it was never known to them that he would indeed grow up to become 'the world's youngest general.' The boy was none other than General Kaito Sukhai: the one who led thousands of Naga soldiers armed with loyalty, self-belief and a handful of weapons who embarked on a gallant mission to liberate the Nagas from the hands of overwhelming oppressors.

This book unfolds the tale of a real-life hero who was born in between the two world wars and eventually became infatuated with military bearings from his very young age. Growing up, he sensed the political disorder in which his people were embroiled, after the British ended their colonial occupation in South-East Asia. Naga Hills was then forcefully divided into two regions at the international boundary of Burma and India, against the desire of the Nagas who were deprived of free will and left reeling under the siege of Indian military regime. Kaito, still in his teenage years, took a solemn pledge to defend his people from this alien incursion.

The story becomes even more interesting when this young leader creates his own army, by training and transforming the distraught Naga peasants into a lethal army to fight against the greater adversary in an attempt to re-claim their long-seized self-determination. The trials and suffering endured during this struggle are unrivalled. The spine-chilling saga while procuring weapons and training to fight against the formidable odds is mesmerizing. Some of General Kaito Sukhai's audacious feats can be seen in the first Indo-Naga battle which took place at Hoshepu village, Zunheboto, where he fought the legions of Indian Rajputs with merely 16 Naga Safe Guards and some volunteers. In the aftermath of this battle, he took hundreds of Indian Rajput's soldiers' lives at the cost of five brave soldiers. His brilliant feats and bizarrely brave actions surpassed his age and time. About the age of 23, he was given the responsibility of commanding the newly formed Naga National army. And indeed, this young general transformed this tiny Naga army into a deadly force. He was one of the greatest military commanders of his time, because consistently, for almost a decade, he led the diminutive but no-less-spirited army to resist and fight against the powerful Indian military troops. An optimist, Kaito always looked at the world through rose-coloured glasses. He defied the limit of practicality, by trekking into one of the most fortified frontiers in the world (the Indo-Pakistan border) with an elite batch of 150 soldiers, to obtain weapons and military training.

It was not the best training or his educational qualification that made him such a formidable general, it was the natural charisma, agility, innate courage and stout dedication that qualified him to be the youngest military General in the annals of the world. Many commentators did rightly define him as the 'born General' and 'the youngest commander-in-chief'. The Naga National Movement was the mother of armed struggle in India. This was the first armed revolt that paved the way for many other such conflicts, in North-East India, and General Kaito Sukhai was the one who launched this armed revolt against the Indian armed forces. He displayed outstanding courage and remarkable leadership abilities throughout his life. He faced many perils and efficiently swept aside colossal barriers, and brought in to light, the Naga freedom movement, in an incredible stand.

His passion for Naga independence is analogous to an inflated balloon pining for a sky. When the Indo-Naga talks were in gridlock and the political accord of the Nagas was submerged in disunity, General Kaito Sukhai ultimately formed an Army Government in Nagaland to save the Naga Movement, which was on the verge of collapse. However, unfortunately, some people misinterpreted his strategy and shot him on August 3, 1968 at Kohima. General Kaito Sukhai succumbed to this injury and died on 4 August 1968, bringing to a tragic end the life of one of the most brilliant commanders of all time.

Some may wonder why a thrilling story such as this has been in the dark for long. In recent years, many writers did try to highlight the legend of this young leader, but they failed in the effort. It may have been because they could not garner much information or it could be the lack of intact printed material on General Kaito Sukhai, since most of his works were either destroyed or lost in the conflict between the two warring groups. Back then, there was a massive curb on Naga insurgency by the Indian army and merely an utterance of the word 'Naga freedom fighters' could land a person behind bars or have him questioned rigorously, which apparently daunted many from pursuing and exploring such a fascinating story. Another delay in writing this story could be the remoteness of his birthplace which caused most writers to end up visiting the State capital Kohima and not Kaito's native place Zunheboto, which is hundreds of kilometres from Kohima. Finally, Dr. Kuhoi Zhimomi, General Kaito's youngest brother along with Khekaho Zhimomi decided to author a complete and factual account of the life of General Kaito Sukhai.

The book will hopefully dispel the misconception some people had regarding the formation of the Naga Army Government. The narrative underscores the extraordinary feats of this young gentlemen which had beset even the formidable nemesis. It is an effort to record General Kaito's legacy for the generations to come. Above all, it tries to shed a light on how the past Naga leaders put a whole-hearted effort into transforming the fraught Nagas into a nation of free people.

One

The birth of a legend

Range upon range of misty mountains extending from North-West Myanmar to the Sub-Himalayan frontiers of North-East India form an area known as 'The Himalayan Triangle', where the three great nations – India, China, and Myanmar[1] – meet. As this remote hilly area is predominantly inhabited by around sixty tribes and sub-tribes of the people known as Nagas, the region has also been called 'the Naga Hills'. The place of origin of the Nagas is disputed. Some scholars believe that the Nagas originated from an area between the Yangtze and the Yellow River in Northwest China, but there are also other narratives. Legends around the migration of many Naga tribes refer to a place called Makhel as their place of dispersal. Makhel is a small village in what is now Senapati district, about ten miles south-east of Kohima, the State capital of Nagaland.

In the mid-19th century, when the British arrived in the Naga Hills, it was an uncharted vastness, a rugged extent of deep jungles, hostile to outsiders. However, when the British took leave in 1947, this territory was regrettably carved between different political entities. Today the Naga Hills are divided by the international boundary between Myanmar and India. In the Far East, Mount Saramati, snow-capped in winter, stands at 3,840 meters above sea level, while in the north-east, at 3,040 metres above sea level, Mount Japfu looms magnificently

---
1 Formerly Burma.

over hundreds of lesser hills. The Naga Hills are blessed with fertile lands and a lush forested landscape, with an abundance of cascading freshwater streams. These hills are now the abode of about 3.5 million Naga people, who had a certain notoriety among the British because of their reputation for head-hunting in the past. This practice, which had complex cultural significance, was gradually brought to an end with the start of the British Administration in the late nineteenth century and the advent of the American Christian Missionaries around the same time. The arrival of Christianity heralded the start of a new way of life for many Naga communities. Although the adoption of the new religion was slow, at first, it gathered momentum, and education began to steer the Naga communities towards Christian values and the modern world.

The rich culture, innate artistry, stunning textiles, colourful festivals, and famously cheerful nature of the Naga people have long delighted the visitors who were lucky enough to reach these hills. Lying at the core of the current state of Nagaland, Zunheboto is the headquarters of the Sümi tribe. It once rejoiced in the title 'Land of Warriors', owing to the fact that the Sümis, along with most other Naga tribes, were known for head-hunting in pre-Christian days. The Sümi warriors, in particular, were known for their agility, audacity and fierceness. It is an odd irony that today the largest monumental church in Asia stands tall at Zunheboto, the abode of the people who, only a century ago, were considered the most dreaded war-hawks.

In November 1885, when the British regime in the Naga Hills was at its peak, Sukhai, the Chief from the Zhimomi clan, invaded dozens of villages that had already acceded to the British alliance policy and he severed seventy-six heads and took them home as trophies. Inevitably, this aroused the wrath of the British. The authorities declare war on Sukhai. However valiant and fearless Sukhai and his warriors were, their traditional weapons could not match the guns of the British, and so he had to reluctantly admit defeat.

As quoted in the diaries of British officials, in the State Archive, Sukhai was imposed a fine of two *mithuns* (bison) ten cattle, thirty *daos* (machetes) and hundred spears (traditional weapons). The measure akin to a king's ransom, in those days, was paid as compensation for the trouble he meted towards the British subjects. Then, on 1st April, 1887, as a punishment for his pride, Sukhai was sent off to Kohima for detention.

During his confinement, Sukhai haughtily refused to take meals from the white people; he instead chose to constantly gulp down 'axuthuzu' tobacco juice from his tobacco jar without eating food. The British officials began to panic. Sukhai was the Chief from the most powerful clan in the region and if he died under their custody, there would be a huge uproar and mayhem. Therefore, to avoid such a situation, Sukhai had to be well looked after and the British had no choice but to permit the Sümis to bring in food for their Chief. The officials were utterly amazed by the amount of reverence Sukhai commanded among his subjects. More than forty individuals presented with platters laden with different Naga delicacies: meat of various animals, fish of different species and sizes, and cooked rice of different colours arrived at Kohima to nourish their leader. The British realised that if such lavishness was required to look after the Sümi Chief, then it was evident that they could not keep Sukhai in custody for long. After this event, unlike the other prisoners who were prone to be ill-treated, Sukhai was treated with respect and given the luxuries appropriate for any Naga chief.

Sukhai was released from custody after a two-month confinement. At the time of his release, the British officials, as a token of peace and goodwill, presented him with a red blanket. This red fabric shawl is usually worn by the Naga chiefs, and was introduced by the British to signify the status of the Naga chiefs. It has been said that Sukhai, the great-grandfather of General Kaito Sukhai, was among the first Sümi chiefs to be bestowed with a red blanket by the British administration. Before he left, they said, "Sukhai, go and rule your people as you have in the past." He was sent off in an atmosphere of cordiality and, thereafter, a warm affinity existed between Sukhai and the British administrators.

About 30 years after that episode, the First World War began, and the Nagas, as well as other peoples, within the British Empire, were obliged to provide manpower for the Allies. Sukhai's second son (Kaito's grand-uncle) Kuhoi Sema Naga was chosen to lead about 2,000 Naga Labour Corps men to France. On 21 April, 1917 they left for Marseille to assist the Allies on the Western frontier. As fate would have it, Kuhoi Sema Naga died during the course of the Great War and was buried in Marseilles, France.

(Dated Kohima, the 30th September 1995, NO. HOME/SCTA-16/94: The Governor of Nagaland is pleased to decide that the name 'Sümi' shall replace 'Sema' with immediate effect. Henceforth, the name Sümi shall be used in all official and non-official correspondence.)[2]

Naga participants who returned after the end of this Great War undoubtedly became the pioneers of modern Naga politics and culture. For the Western world, the First World War was a period of despair and anguish, but for the Nagas, who had never previously ventured beyond their traditional boundaries and went to serve in Europe, it was a journey of discovery into unfamiliar realms. Their affiliation and experiences with the Western world acted as a catalyst for major change in Naga society. Among the insights they acquired through their experiences was an understanding of politics, which they discussed with their people, immediately, upon their return from the West. In October 1918, very soon after the Corps return, an integrated Naga organization known as The Naga Club was formed. Ten years later, in January, 1929, this organization submitted a

---

2 Prior to the year 1995, Sumi people are known as Sema but after passing out this order on 30th September 1995 they were henceforth known as Sumi and they started using Sumi in every official purpose

memorandum to the Simon Commission demanding that the Nagas should be left out of the reformed scheme of administration that the Commission was considering for British India and left as they were before the arrival of the British. Despite this petition, unfortunately, the Naga Hills, without the people's consent, was severed and split between the Union of India and Myanmar, when the British took leave of the sub-continent.

For the Nagas, the memorandum to the Simon Commission was the Magna Carta of Naga political rights. This memorandum was the crucible wherein the Naga self-determination movement was forged and the Naga political challenge has persisted, unresolved for nearly a century. Indeed, it is one of the world's oldest political gridlocks.

The ideas and principles of Naga political rights were based on the contents of this memorandum and this is how and where the journey of the Naga independence movement began. Three decades after this event, and after many disagreements among the Naga leaders, the brothers Kaito Sukhai and Kughato Sukhai stepped into their ancestors' footsteps to lead the quest to free the Nagas from a forced foreign regime.

About 20 kilometres away from the Sümi headquarters, Zunheboto, on the southern flank of a great rough foothill, lies a small but beautiful village called Ghukhuyi, which still shows the traces of past valour. It was established in the late 19th century by two brothers, Ghukhuyi and Hokiye, with the blessing of their father, Sukhai Zhimomi, the Chief of Sukhai village. General Kaito was the grandson of Hokiye and the great-grandson of Sukhai. When the call came to protect the Nagas from foreign dominion, this tiny village offered more resistance than many others pooled together. Naga leaders like General Kaito Sukhai, his eldest brother Kughato Sukhai, the second Ato Kilonser (Prime Minister) Federal Government of Nagaland, Gen. Zuheto Swu, the G.O.C Eastern Command, Naga army; Major Zheluto Awomi, the first batch of the Naga Army and myriad other Naga national-freedom fighters are the offspring of this tiny but significant village.

Born into an affluent Sümi Naga family of the Zhimomi clan, Kaito Sukhai was the second son of Kuhoto Zhimomi and Kiholi Yepthomi (the eldest daughter of Kuhozu Yepthomi, the Chief of Sukhalu village). Kuhoto Zhimomi was the chief of Ghukhuyi village. He served as *Dobashi* (interpreter), Kohima Division from 1921 to 1948.

He was one of the few Nagas to be awarded the B.E.M (British Empire Medal), in 1945, for meritorious service rendered to the Allied forces in the WWII. During the British regime, Dobashi (interpreter) was the most prestigious government job an individual Naga could hold and Kuhoto was fortunate to have been appointed to this post. Kuhoto and Kiholi had five sons and four daughters – Kughato, Toshili, Hotoli, Hoshili, Kaito, Vikuto, Vitoli, Phoishe, and Kuhoi. Kuhoto's firstborn, Kughato Sukhai, served as the second Prime Minister, Federal Government of Nagaland, from 1958 to 1968 and Hotoli Swu, the third child, was married to Scato Swu, the second President of the Federal Government of Nagaland. It is said that some of Kaito's distinctive traits were inherited from his great-grandfather Sukhai, the aforementioned warrior Chief of Sukhai village and his grand-uncle Kuhoi Sema Naga, the outstanding warrior who led around 2,000 Nagas to France.

Right from his mother's womb, Kaito displayed a demeanour unlike other children, and his mother Kiholi felt that something was going to be different about this son. His father Kuhoto, through his work as a Dobashi, knew the ins-and-outs of the Naga Hills and was acquainted with many people, including a seer named Alemtemjen Ao from Longsa village, Mokokchung District. The seer was renowned for his prophetic abilities, hence, prior to Kaito's birth, Kuhoto called him to Ghukhuyi village. The seer told Kuhoto and Kiholi that a son would be born to them and numerous people would follow him. The parents were so elated with the seer's prophesy that they sent him off with a huge sum of money.

One sunny day in early summer, on 22 May 1933, as expected by the parents, and true to the seer's prediction, a fair and healthy boy who was to make his mark on history, was born to the elated couple. Their felicity knew no bounds and the parents proudly named him Kai-to, which means 'reign to victory' or 'reign to win' where 'Kai' connotes 'reign' and 'to' refers to 'win' or 'victory'. From the time he began to crawl, unique characteristics began to show, including extraordinary tenacity and inflexibility. He would direct the person carrying him to take him wherever he wanted to go. Going against his wishes would make him so livid that he would pull that person's hair viciously.

Life with his brothers and sisters was full of adventure and affection. There was a significant age gap between the sons Kughato, Kaito and Vikuto. Kughato was eight years older than Kaito, while Vikuto was two years younger than Kaito; yet, they were close friends as well as siblings. The rapport between the siblings and their courtesy towards other people can be largely attributed to their parents, who had both descended from well-respected families. While the children's upbringing was full of love and affection, the values of honour and integrity, and the skills of leadership were deeply instilled in them. In addition, they were made aware of the worth of education and its importance in the rapidly changing world. One evening after dinner, Kuhoto gathered his five younger children around the kitchen fireplace. The three eldest – Kughato, Toshili and Hoshili – were not there. Kughato and Toshili were already married and had their own homes and children to look after, while, sadly, Hoshili had died. On this occasion, Kuhoto assured his five children...

> *"Whoever among you would be first to qualify Class VIII shall be given the privilege to study in Shillong."*

In those days Shillong was considered the ultimate destination for any education-seeking student from Northeast-India, and only the affluent families from the region were able to send their children there. As promised by their father, the privilege was given to Vikuto, for he was the first among the five younger children to pass Class VIII, making the grade even before Kaito.

Kaito's brother, Vikuto Zhimomi, was born in the year 1935; an alumnus of Government High School Shillong, he graduated in 1965. Depending only on his own means, Vikuto served the Naga people throughout his life. He was the second President of the Naga *Gaon buras* Federation (a confederacy of Naga Chieftains) for 10 years. Currently, he is the Chairman of the collective forum of Naga Chieftains and Naga *Dobashis* Federation. A forlorn look passes over his elderly face on mention of his late brother's name, but nostalgia fills the air as Vikuto recounts his childhood years with Kaito. A soft-spoken man, Vikuto is now in his late-80s and his frail figure and grey hair reveal his age. In an unhurried manner, he settles with dignity into his chair and looks pensive as he starts to recall the past. Although the two brothers were different in build, Vikuto was tall and lanky, while Kaito was short and spruce, Vikuto's chiselled face has more than a reflection of his handsome brother Kaito.

From his childhood days and throughout his life, Kaito stood out among his equals. He was decisive and always spoke his mind, without shame or fear. If someone found fault with him or made fun of his ignorance, he simply ignored them and made his tormentors feel as if they didn't exist. In the face of trouble, he would remain calm and unperturbed, and resolve the matter sensibly. He preferred cold food over warm meals. He also abstained from chewing tobacco because a repeated hiccup had troubled him when last he tried it. He seldom drank local rice brew and abstained from any other alcoholic beverages. One amusing fact was that people assumed he indulged in alcohol but he would just pretend to be drinking and would secretly spill the contents of his glass, which always ended the session, with what we commonly call 'an excellent Dutch bargain.'

Nothing could dampen Kaito's spirit or deter his aspirations. He was a giant in leadership abilities and committed to excellence. His peers were awed by his wit and dexterity. His bodily and mental reflexes were equally impressive. He had fits of temper but never lost control. Subtle, skilful, vigorous, adventurous, curious and agile was Kaito. He was quite stern towards his playmates, especially if they were not as energetic as he. Even as a child, he would frequently give orders and tasks to his friends. For instance, he would order them to gather a number of pebbles for slingshots within a count of ten, and if anyone failed to follow his order within the fixed time, that particular kid would receive a severe reprimand and, even worse, a kick on the buttock. Vikuto recalls how his brother Kaito would whack him many times on a given day; he would blubber not less than ten times a day because he was not nimble like Kaito. But, despite Kaito's stringent nature to Vikuto, they were like Siamese twins, always inseparable. If either of them was gone, for a day or two, they would yearn for each other's company.

Regardless of Kaito's toughness toward his brother and his lazy friends, at the end of the day, he overlooked the entire daytime activities and showered his affection on one and all. His kindness and affection were always genuine.

Kaito had distinctive qualities, possibly attributable to the fact that his parents had told him about the prophecy that he would become a renowned leader, which made him believe that he had a unique calling. His self-belief was unyielding, even in the face of criticism and distrust. Thus, he assumed he was the top of his cohort and that his plan was necessarily better than anyone else's, proving himself right on many occasions. Kaito saw the world in a different way: he thought out-of-the-box and unleashed trailblazing ideas. He was much more likely to follow his own instinct than to incline to others' opinion. He strongly believed that a man is the master of his destiny; and that a person should strive hard to carve out his niche in life.

In the early 1940s, when Great Britain and Japan were at war; his father Kuhoto was serving under C.R. Pawsey, Deputy Commissioner of Naga Hills, Kohima Division. Kaito and Vikuto were 8 and 6 years old, respectively. Kuhoto instructed his two young boys:

> *"A group of Japanese soldiers will be coming to the village in search of the Allied forces, so keep vigil with your mother and when they arrive, help your mother to serve them food right away. You must know that further hassles can be subdued in full stomach."*

Kuhoto was going into hiding along with his eldest son, Kughato. Then a robust teenager, Kughato was clad in a British-issued garment, the only clothes available in the Hills other than the traditional loincloth; therefore, there was a strong chance that the Japanese soldiers might take him for an allied informer and beat him up, which they usually did.

It was late in the afternoon when the boys, who were guarding their cattle in the meadows, saw five weary soldiers marching into the village. As fast as their little legs could carry them, they ran towards their home, which stood on a hillock. Their house was grander than others in the village and had more adornments. It was a typical Naga chieftain's home, embellished with animal horns, spears, machetes, and various intricate designs on the façade. Neither the Japanese nor any other visitor would have any difficulty identifying the house of the village Chief. Their mother, who never hesitated to feed hungry travellers passing through their village, was busy instructing her servants inside the kitchen when the boys rushed in to inform her about the arrival of the Japanese soldiers. As the soldiers were approaching the gates, the kids, along with their mother, hurried towards the gate to greet the soldiers. They did not forget their father's instruction, "Treat them kindly and feed them well lest they may harm you". As expected, the khaki-clad Japanese entered the gate and in rather harsh tones accompanied with hand signals, asked them tersely, "Where are the British soldiers?" The mother and the kids couldn't grasp the language but could understand their gestures, so they replied, "They're not here".

The soldiers searched every corner of the house until they were satisfied. Worn out by their long journey, they threw their weapons carelessly on the ground and sat down to rest. The two young brothers, adhering to their father's instruction, tried their best not to aggravate the Japanese soldiers; and with all the courtesy they could muster, they rushed to and fro helping their mother serve food to the soldiers. The boys watched with some amusement as the hungry soldiers devoured their food with evident satisfaction. After the meal, the soldiers sat down and explained how the Japanese and Nagas look alike and therefore must help each other. "We are going to shoot the white people," said the Japanese soldiers. They also inquired whether there were sick people in the village for they had brought lots of medicine. Kaito and Vikuto ran about the village and announced:

> *"The Japanese soldiers are not going to hurt anyone, they have brought medicine too, so come out and get treated."*

Prior to the arrival of Japanese soldiers almost the entire village had been hiding in the nearby jungle. One by one, the relieved villagers started to pour out.

> *"They gave us lots of medicines for different types of illness and left for Kohima to participate in the great battle which was in the offing, recollected Vikuto."*

General Kaito had an innate inclination for military life. His adventurous early days were fully directed towards military pursuits and leadership. As a matter of fact, his entire life was mostly devoted to military activities. Those who knew him, remember that he was never alone, he would always keep a band of 20 to 30 boys aged around 10 to 12, whom he called his Children's Army. It was way too early for a child of his age to keep a band of boys at his disposal almost all the time. People must have assumed that this was just a self-indulgent boy's game, yet to him, it was no child's game, and maybe he really knew what he was doing. None could have guessed that the future General was in fact disciplining his followers for battles to come.

J.P. Vikugha, who formerly served as the Lt. Colonel and Commander of Signal Corps Naga Army, now in his early 80s, vividly remembers how he enrolled into Kaito's Children's Army as Captain. He obtained a great deal of experience from this, which benefited him in his later military career. For his Children's Army, Kaito would select only those boys who were daring, mischievous, restless, and aggressive in nature; the placid and slow children had no place in his Army. The chosen boys were then made to undergo training such as climbing trees, running across the hills, playing tug-of-war, fencing, wrestling, crawling inside the jungles and many other physical tests. These methods would build up their strength and stamina. His orders were respected and followed by all the children. The slightest noncompliance with his commands would attract severe punishment, such as carrying heavy loads on one's back and running non-stop for a mile or so. For the battle drills, the Children's Army would be divided into two groups. The leaders then led their respective groups to the appointed battle ground, where Kaito would supervise military-like combat drills and record the performances of each fighting troop. The objective of the exercise was to strategize the attack and capture the whole area of the battle ground. At the end of the game, the result was declared and the winners were rewarded with sweets and other such favours.

The defeated group would be encouraged to win in the next round by doing more exercises. These above methods were learnt from the allied soldiers who were stationed at Kaito's village.

During the Second World War, the British Allied forces had set a camp at his village. At every opportunity, he would hang around with the Allied soldiers so that he could learn more about military life. One day, the camp Commander asked him to fetch some water. Kaito in turn ordered his boys to fetch the water, while he hung about with the commander. The boys without hesitation brought the water, put it in front of the Commander and stood obediently in an army formation. After a while, the little boss ordered his boys to parade out of the camp. In another incident, to check the competence of the children, the same Commander offered Kaito and his boys the chance to test fire a rifle inside the trench. No one except Kaito was bold enough to accept the offer. The Allied personnel watching the scene were amazed by the way he picked the rifle without hesitation and was about to fire, but then the Commander stopped him from doing so. The Allied soldiers remarked that the boy would one day grow up to be an excellent soldier but never knew that indeed he would grow up to become the world's youngest General.

Kaito knew that education was essential if he were to be a great leader in the modern era. However, his passion for military life remained far greater than his enthusiasm for academic pursuits. Despite a conscious effort to focus on his education, his performance in school gradually declined. His school reports were not favourable, and his frequent bursts of anger and his unpredictable nature antagonised friends and teachers alike. Kaito was the blue-eyed child in the family, and his arrogance was understood only by his formative considerate teachers, who in most cases, ignored his wrongdoings. When he was in Class four, at Atukuzu High School, Kaito had not prepared well for an exam, so he brought a Japanese sword from home and kept the blade beside him. His intention was obvious: If his teachers caught him cheating, he knew that the sight of the sword would prevent them from approaching him. His teachers were plainly infuriated and astonished at such behaviour from a very young student. Kaito started his lower primary at Atukuzu (now Satakha, Zunheboto District) but, in 1944, along with his elder sister Hotoli, he was sent to Mission School Kohima. However, events on a world scale were soon to interrupt his schooling and change the Naga Hills forever.

The year was 1944 and WWII was at its peak, Japanese troops had breached India's North-Eastern flank with the aim of preventing a re-invasion of Burma. Troops from the Indian National Army accompanied them, and some in Japanese High Command dreamed of driving the British from the sub-continent. With great difficulty, the Allied Forces prevented the Japanese from capturing Kohima and marching on to the railhead at Dimapur, replete with supplies and military hardware. Small as it was, Kohima became the main gateway to Britain's Indian Empire; losing it could have ended the already declining British Raj reign. Although the damage and losses were great, the Allies managed to repel the Japanese in an encounter that could have been their worst military tragedy. Kohima became a mammoth war theatre: thousands of soldiers were slaughtered, on both sides, the town was razed to the ground, and the populace was severely affected. The epitaph in the Kohima War Cemetery reads

> **When you go home, tell them of us and say we gave our today, for your tomorrow.**

Indeed, the National War Museum in the UK has awarded the battle of Kohima and Imphal the title of 'Britain's Greatest Battle', ahead of the Normandy Landings and Waterloo.

The War inevitably meant that Kaito and his sister Hotoli had to discontinue their studies at Mission School Kohima. And so, in 1945, they re-joined the other siblings at Atukuzu. Kaito continued his education at Satakha and, thereafter, completed Class VII at Zunheboto Government High School. During his stay in Satakha, he was the Group Commander of the Boy Scouts and, whenever the school inspector or any other dignitaries visited the school, he would receive the guests courteously, fully clad in Sümi traditional attire.

This glimpse of the childhood and early life of Kaito Sukhai gives us more than a hint of his extraordinary innate abilities and points to the path he was destined to tread.

Sukhai Zhimomi the chief of Sukhai village and General Kaito's great- grandfather.
Photo credit: J.P. Mills Photo Archive 'Sukhai at Sukhalu village,' photo dated: 1919

THE FORGOTTEN HERO
Kuhoi Sema Naga lies buried at the Commonwealth War Graves Commission cemetery at Mazargues in Marseilles, France. Also known as Kuhoi Zhimomi, he was the son of Naga Chief Sukhai Zhimomi. What makes him special, says Peter Francis, spokesperson of the CWGC, is that the original temporary grave marker (above) for Kuhoi recorded that he took 24 heads and was present at the death of 130 enemies in battle.

Image on right - The acronym 'CWGC' is Commonwealth War Graves Commission. Kuhoi Sema Naga, the Chief of the Naga Labour Corp who went to serve the war on western frontier of France in WWI died in Marseille, France, 25th December 1917. He was the grand-uncle of General Kaito Sukhai. Above is his grave marking and Epitaph.

General Kaito's parents Kuhoto and Kiholi Zhimomi

Two

The initial years

In February 1950, in an attempt to prevent the Naga Hills from being forced to merge with India, the Naga National Council (NNC) declared it would hold a plebiscite. The Indian Government was, however, against this proposal and began describing the NNC as the 'Voice of the misguided few.' Nevertheless, the NNC remained firm in its commitment and on 16 May 1951, under the leadership of A.Z. Phizo, the fourth NNC President, the Nagas conducted a voluntary plebiscite to affirm that they desired to be left on their own as they had been before the arrival of the British. The result was staggering, 99.9% of the Nagas declared that they would not live under Indian rule.

The Nagas' perception of their history was critical in determining the Plebiscite result. They had no recollection or memories of ever being under the influence of any nation or ruler. From their viewpoint, they had been independent from time immemorial, free of any form of bondage, and distinctive in their culture. The Naga Plebiscite was, therefore, a means to convey to the Indian Union and the international community, that, although the Nagas had, by force of circumstances, become entwined with India, after the British left, they never had been, and never wanted to be a part of the Indian Union. It is a sad fact that India did not deem the Naga Plebiscite worthy of note and ignored it. Had it been valued; the Naga national movement could have seen some tangible outcome.

In early 1951, Kaito, still a teenager, joined the mainstream of the Naga nationalists – the NNC. After becoming involved in the Naga Movement, he worked hard and earnestly for its growth. The Plebiscite documents were carried all over the Naga Hills, apart from the Tuensang Hills Un-administered Area and the Naga Hills of North-West Myanmar. The Naga Youth Wing, under NNC's direction, took on the role of supervising the Plebiscite. In this undertaking, Kaito was extremely active and supervised the Plebiscite initiative over the entire Sümi region. Accompanied by his younger brother Vikuto, a number of Vikuto's classmates, and Visheto of Hoshepu, he took on the massive task of travelling on foot throughout the Sümi-occupied lands, to collect the votes in the form of signatures and thumb impressions. The collected votes were then submitted to the President of the Youth Wing of the Naga National Council. On 28 May, 1951, after submission of the votes, Kaito's companion, Visheto, was imprisoned at Zunheboto Police station. He became the first person among the Nagas to be imprisoned for active involvement in the Naga Plebiscite. Kaito, however, managed to evade capture and went on the run.

The Naga Plebiscite was heavily condemned by the Indian government and what followed later was a frenzied assault on the Plebiscite organizers by Indian authorities. Legal actions were taken against the initiators and a massive manhunt for NNC leaders was launched. It was a chilling winter evening in 1952, when the Assam rifles concentrated the entire community of the town of Zunheboto, at the local football ground. They threatened them of dire consequences should they continue to participate in or encourage any further anti-national activities. In the midst of this fearful situation, the impression Kaito made that day was profound. He stood up from amongst the massive gathering and shouted for Naga independence. He dared the youths to come forward to fight and sacrifice their lives for the cause of Naga freedom. In response to his call, 37 youths stood up daringly and volunteered to follow him. They were willing to fight for the cause, even to the extent of sacrificing their lives. That day, Kaito exploded into a burning fury, reflecting a wrath which had been mounting up inside his heart during the previous few years. The young lad had a total loathing of the ill-treatment meted to his people. As he proclaimed for Naga independence, he wasn't surprised that throngs of youths would rose up in solidarity with him. He knew that those youths themselves or their families had been subjected to similar situations to those which Kaito had seen and experienced.

Observing the patriotic sentiments running high among the detained crowd, the Indian armed forces thought it best to disperse them. After that event, bearing in mind the gravity of Kaito's rabble-rousing calls to the youths, the Indian troops embarked on a rigorous operation to arrest the young leader and his friends. However, Kaito eluded the attempt, by the Indian authorities, to capture him. Typically, Kaito would calculate what might occur, and would execute his move in advance, which is why it was hard to pin him down. But how many times or how long could he and his followers sustain the constant harrying of Indian troops? And now, cowering in fear of enemy's might was not his intention.

The moment those youths stood up with him on that fateful day, Kaito's expectation soared high with hope like an iridescent sky. Complementing the support of the youth, Kaito also gained unconditional support from the local populace. Nagas have long since been silenced. With a train of woes and miseries constantly dominating the Naga Hills, their cry was:

> *"Why not now? Why do we not meet their challenge? We must show them what we have become, now our free will is at stake."*

Leading a posse of prey and striking back at a massive pack of wolves was a daunting task, but the burden rested on Kaito at that juncture. It would take a lot of intimidation to prevent him and nothing could overcome his will to retaliate against the intruders, supported by an abused horde of prey. Fighting for his nation would become his choice and this intense commitment of Kaito would spiral into an armed movement, and create the rift which persists to this day.

Kaito was infuriated because the Plebiscite, which the NNC, under Phizo, diligently carried out, with the mass public support, was practically ignored. The credential proof of Plebiscite lay wasted in the Indian government closet, like a dusty forgotten manuscript. Although young, Kaito could comprehend that if the Plebiscite had failed to have any positive effect, it was obvious that dialogue alone could not shift the stance of India. What was required was a blend of sound political discourse enhanced by strong-armed resistance, which eventually would impose the Naga perspective on the patronizing approach of the Prime Minister Jawaharlal Nehru and his cabinet colleagues. Nevertheless, until then, as far as Kaito's tiny resisting force was concerned, its action would be limited to self-defence. However, the moral code was clear; Nagas could not be a hounded prey to an outsider on their own soil.

Being constrained by such aforesaid factors, Kaito felt the impulse to procure arms and ammunition for which he required a substantial amount of funding. The challenge was how he could raise the necessary money required. He decided to venture on foodstuff trading. His father being the Chief of the village held a large portion of farm land in the region, while he was also privileged enough to have 32 labourers at his disposal, to till his fields. Besides, Kuhoto was also employed as Dobashi (translator) at the Deputy Commissioner's office in Kohima and was well salaried. This allowed Kuhoto, the advantage of not having to rely on agricultural returns alone. His parents' deriving an abundant quantity of harvest from cultivation made Kaito think that the easiest way to acquire money would be by selling off his parents' products to neighbouring villages and towns. In fact, his parents had to sacrifice their yearlong stocks to feed the Naga soldiers. They would feed the Naga fighters for weeks and months. "I bear in mind how Kaito's mother provided us a granary filled to the brim with rice on more than one occasion." says Hopong, the first Tribal council President of Yimchunger tribe and the first Angh (Governor) of Free Naga region. With the consent of his parents, Kaito started selling beans, chilies, gingers, soya beans, etc. Good fortune befell Kaito and he made a considerable turnover from the trade. With the money raised, he purchased arms and ammunition, and smuggled them secretly into his village. Goods were transported on four ponies owned by his parents through the old British road via Chouzuba from Kohima.

Most of the weapons he acquired were from Kohima town and nearby places. A good many were sourced from old dumps left behind by the British and Japanese forces after the WWII. Some of them had been unused for quite a time and needed to be repaired. The guns and bullets were brought to his village and kept in secret hideouts. During this entire episode, Zuheto Swu and Kaito Sukhai were as thick as thieves; Zuheto accompanied Kaito during the process of purchasing and smuggling weapons. Back in their village, the folks called the duo by the name 'Xusavi' which means 'the naughty ones'. Zuheto Swu would promptly become the obvious successor of Kaito Sukhai in the Naga military hierarchy. The defective guns were repaired by a hard-working revamping team headed by a skilled hand, Hakhezu of Hoishe village, and readied arms stocks were guarded by Kaito's trusted men. Kaito's intention was now apparent: he was already preparing his personal army. Perhaps not in leaps and bounds, but his followers were growing by day, a force much loyal to reckon with. From what we could clearly infer from the above fact is that Naga arms movement had an extremely modest beginning, because the tender shoot of Naga army had solely germinated from sheer sweats and toils of Naga peasants.

The year of 1952 and early 1953 saw a lot of events occur in the Naga Hills. In January, 1952, the NNC launched a civil disobedience campaign, refusing to pay taxes and boycotting India's first ever general election. On October 18, 1952, Zasibito Nagi was killed at Kohima, during a protest march. On March 30, 1953, Nehru, accompanied by her young daughter, Indira Gandhi, and Burmese premier U Nu, also known as Thakin Nu, arrived at Kohima to assess the situation in the Naga Hills. By mid-1953 NNC was on a campaigning mission to garner supports for the Naga National movement. Meanwhile, Kaito knew he had to tread the hard way and so, after having prepared his small band of avant-garde militia, on his home turf, he was now anxious to expand his group into a lethal guardian of the Naga people. He was of the strong opinion that some pragmatically taught fighters were required amidst his newly founded group. Although a squad not to be taken likely, the first cohort of his army was largely raised from amongst loyalists and farmers. He had to reach out to enlist some qualified soldiers.

The urge that had been driving Kaito since childhood days was categorically getting into shape. It was the onset of 1953 when Kaito went to Mission High school in Shillong to pursue his higher studies. The real purpose, however, was not study, it was something else. The child prodigy who was just out of his teens had already primed a blueprint inside his mind. Shillong being one of the educational hubs that outclassed others in North-East India, many privileged students from the region, including Nagas, were studying there. After his arrival, under the ruse of learning, Kaito tirelessly organised a network and brought the Naga Nationalistic ideology to Naga students, as well as Naga recruits of Assam Regiment, Happy Valley Shillong. He encouraged them to bond in the ambit of Naga Nationalism and fight for their inherent rights.

Kaito being a devoted sportsman, excelled in badminton, was a natural in karate, played football, and also loved archery. Thus, his days in Shillong were dotted with all sparkles and colours and he was honoured with the King Scout award for his achievements in sport. His political campaign progressed until, unluckily, his undercover acts were exposed by the Indian Intelligence sleuths who had been on his tail. His stay at Shillong was ended. But it was a fruitful stay, during which he engendered a huge momentum among the educated Nagas in Shillong. During the short span, he was able to persuade an adequate number of Nagas, including students, to join the Indian army, so that after being trained, they could come back to Naga Hills and train others, to defend the future of the Naga people. In fact, a number of those who had been influenced by Kaito's advocacy, deserted the Indian military service and returned to join his group.

In the early winter of 1954, Kaito came back from Shillong and started assembling a bunch of troublesome and wayward youths. In the local dialect, these people were referred to as 'Boltusu', which means 'the vagabonds'. Kaito influenced them to bond into his armed group, and then he initiated his scheming activities at Dimapur. December 5, 1954, could be reckoned as the defining moment in the history of the Naga armed resistance movement. Kaito founded a group named the Naga Safe Guard. He recruited twelve people at the launch of this group. The reason why he picked twelve fighters he would later clearly explain. He said:

> *"Jesus led twelve disciples to preach the gospel, which is why I had recruited twelve warriors to lead an Army to defend the Naga people."*

This band would later emerge as the formidable Naga National Army. The twelve fighters were:

1) Yeveto	2) Lhoshezu	3) Tsapiki
4) Zheluto	5) Mithizu	6) Shilon
7) Hothrong	8) Pukhato	9) Viniho
10) Haqhizhe	11) Tsalito	12) Khashepu

In the intervening time, during the fall of winter, 1953, Phizo arrived at Aghunato with some of his NNC members Tolhopu and Luzukhu Sümi. Aghunato, then, was a part of the Naga Hills un-administered zone, which fell under the North East Frontier Agency (NEFA). This area was known as 'the free Naga region', because the area was neither under the former British Administration nor the later Indian Union nor Burma. The NNC had arrived in the region to propagate their objectives concerning the Naga freedom movement. Phizo had already discovered that this Free Naga region could function as a suitable location to break free the rest of the Nagas who were then within the Indian administrative area. A public meeting was held at Viyilho village under Aghunato, which was attended by several village chiefs from the region. Phizo and other leaders who spoke at the gathering were vocal and realistic. The essence of the topic was that Nagas were a unique people, born with intrinsic rights, and, therefore, no outsiders had the right to rule or dictate over the Naga people. Villagers were sternly advised not to be swayed by the Indian government offers of red blankets, free salts, jobs, etc. The people were sternly warned to resist such offers, as accepting those things would certainly pave way for the Indian authorities to impose multiple taxes. Besides, they also cited that men would be forcefully drafted into the Indian military, while, the wives of those who refused to join would be defiled. Taking note of these details, addressees were totally shocked, because all those things, briefed by the speakers, were entirely against the mores and customs of the Naga people. Hence, people present there jointly agreed to support the NNC movement.

Yet again, the following year, in August, 1954, Phizo returned to the free Naga region. He was determined to further encourage the free Naga people to give wider support for the Naga National Movement which was already rooted. Phizo, escorted by two elderly Sümi, Ivulho of Laza and Luzukhu of Baihmo, arrived at Aghunato on August 9. Afterwards, they went to Ngozubo village, which is located not far from Aghunato. Later, that evening, Phizo sent some of his men to

Hukir village to fetch P. Hopong Yimchunger to Ngozubo, Hopong was then the Tribal Council President of Yimchunger tribe. He was also one of the eminent personalities in the free Naga region. The latter arrived at Ngozubo, and prior to meeting with Phizo, Ivulho of Laza raised his hand and apprised Hopong.

Hey Hopong, now I have escorted Phizo to your area, the burden rests on you now to take him around and mobilize for the Naga National Movement.

Ivulho and Luzukhu left Phizo under the care of Hopong and took their leave. The next day, August 10, Hopong took Phizo to his home village of Iponger, where Phizo bluntly told him: "Hopong, it seems India will not heed talks alone, so you have to take up arms and rebel against India."

Hopong was taken aback. He replied: "Phizo, are you serious! The Indian army, even without using guns could trample us. No! It's not possible."

Phizo stated again: "I am a friend of Assam, and you know what that means. We are already under Assam. Literally, we are in jail, so the free Nagas ought to bail us out from the clutches of the Indians."

Hopong then said: "Even if I agree to launch an armed rebellion with India, we do not have any weapons to use against them. Where shall I get weapons?"

Phizo replied: "You will get guns, but you have to buy them."

Hopong snapped back, "We have no money, will you provide us the money?"

Phizo, after a brief silence said: "Maybe you could ask the people to donate it. Why don't you levy two rupees each from every household as a donation."

Hopong thought for a while and said "Well, I'll see to that, but when I start a war will you help me?"

Phizo said "Yes, we will, certainly."

Together, Phizo and Hopong went to Khiamniungan region and campaigned for about a week. After a while, when they became aware of the Indian Army following them, they went their separate ways. Hopong came back to his village and like Phizo advised, he started raising money from the region. By the end of the year he had amassed a substantial sum of money and soon after he went to meet Kaito and procured some weapons from him.

At the beginning of 1955, a bleak situation arose in some parts of the Free Naga areas. Assam police started establishing outposts, at places such as Aghunato, and other locations, in the vicinity. These areas are more particularly occupied by the ramified Eastern Sümis and the Yimchungers. Until then, these people had been unfamiliar with intrusion by strangers, let alone threats and abuse over their lands and their conformist culture. Therefore, when Assam police troops infringed, and brazenly commenced their exploits, in the region, the indigenous community could no longer contain its ethical sentiments and decided that something ought to be done. Intense dislike for Indian soldiers was mounting, in the hearts of the local people. In March, 1955, some Assam Rifles were placed at Hukir village to protect the ongoing alignment of road work between Aghunato and Tuensang. Further, without the consent of villagers, Assam Rifles put up a temporary camp outside the village, by felling bamboos and trees. It wasn't a figment of imagination, as some of them had supposed, not long before, when Phizo had prophesied that such act would occur.

It confirmed the truth of what NNC leaders had predicted earlier. The actions of the Assam Rifles had enraged the villagers and so they waited for the right moment to give a befitting response.

Late on 24th March, 1955, four Assam Rifle personnel entered Hukir village to have their fill of local brew. During the course of having the sips, the Jawans molested a woman. Such was the event Hopong had been awaiting, which allowed him to strike. The villagers flocked together and pounced upon the Jawans, beheaded three of them, while the fourth escaped, but with severe injuries. In the same year, another member of the Assam Rifles was beheaded by the villagers of Kiphire. These incidents were the prelude to a dark season of conflict in the free Naga areas.

Indian forces coming back to avenge their Jawans' death was inevitable. Hopong was troubled by this fact but was reassured by the assurance given to him earlier by Phizo – "Nagas will fight cohesively against any eventualities". His tribesman had done what they had been expected to do. Now the responsibility rested on the NNC leaders and other Naga tribes to shield the Yimchungers from the imminent enemy onslaught. Hopong accordingly relayed a message to NNC President A.Z. Phizo and Naga Home Guards leader Thungti Chang about the situation in which his people were lately enmeshed. Hopong told them that his tribesman had already commenced a war with the Indian troops and as previously agreed, unified assistance must be forthcoming. However, the NNC response was rather tardy and lackadaisical. Hopong was fuming. The NNC President had encouraged him to start a war and then turned a deaf ear to his call. Hopong was in a fix.

Equipped with machetes, spears and a small number of guns, Hopong had faithfully prepared 300 of his brave volunteers to shield his tribe from the impending assault. But would it be even possible? Could a flock of peasants, mostly armed with traditional weapons and a few renovated rifles, defend the tribe from sophisticated trained soldiers equipped with advanced arms? It was not possible.

As expected, on April 18, 1955, Mr. Lakhar APO (Assistant Political Officer) of Aghunato arrived with the Assam Rifles to Hukir village. They set ablaze the entire houses and granaries of the village and shot Mr. Pangchi, the village Chief, to death. The villagers fled to the jungle to hide from the brutality of Indian occupation. Assam Rifles were stationed there for about three days and then returned to Aghunato. Many Yimchungers fled to adjoining Sümi villages, mostly to Ngozubo village. The Assam Rifles, on receiving the news, marched to Ngozubo, on April 30, and burned the whole village to ashes.

The adjoining Sümi villagers were plagued and tortured mercilessly for providing sanctuary to Yimchungers. Once more, the Assam Rifles went to Luvishe village and destroyed the village for no other reason than villagers' helping their Yimchunger brothers. At Luvishe, they killed another Sümi villager named Kiqhezu. The Yimchungers, especially the Huker and Iponger villagers, were rendered helpless. Without foods and shelter they could not hide forever in the jungle. Those villages who sheltered them were penalized heavily by having their granaries set alight, and even, in some instances, being murdered. In the wake of desolation, pain, hunger and panic the villagers were driven out of every hideaway. Yimchungers were left in a most vulnerable state. Fortunately, that was the moment when Kaito appeared on the scene with his group, the Naga Safe Guards.

It is best quoted in the personal words of Hopong Yimchunger:

> *"General Kaito Sukhai saved my tribe from the mass annihilation of Indian Army; I shall be ever grateful to him."*

Kaito by the time had returned from Shillong and was mulishly continuing his passionate calls, from the place which he had left behind, when he relocated to Shillong, years before. No sooner did Kaito hear of the grim situation that had engulfed his brethren than he assembled all he could muster and rushed to the region to defend his Eastern Sümi and Yimchunger brothers from the Indian troops' battering. In April, 1955, Kaito Sukhai arrived at Hoshepu with about a dozen of his finest warriors. Thereafter, they camped at Hoshepu-Khekiye village, which was adjoining to the area of Hukir, the village where the slaying of three Assam Rifles had taken place.

Hopong P Yimchunger was first President of Yimchunger (Yimkhiung) Tribal Council and an Angh (Governor) of the FGN. This grand old man was 110 years when the authors interviewed him on 10 June, 2019. Sadly, he passed away on 16 January, 2021, at the age of 112.

Three

The first Indo-Naga battle

After settling with his followers at Hoshepu, Kaito determined that a well-structured organization must be created to give a strong base to his Safe Guards army, as he was planning to pitch a big battle against a much greater enemy. He called a mass meeting among the Free Naga people, with the assent of the Eastern Sümi Tribal Council (ESTC) executives. ESTC was a ramified organization under the Sümi Tribal Council in the Free Naga Area. ESTC was led by Hutovi of Yemishe and Ghokheto of Khekiye.

Never before had so massive a gathering been held, as the meeting which took place, that fine day, in the early springs of 1955 at Khekiye village. Khekiye was a tiny, enthralling settlement located in the midst of the hilly ranges of Hoshepu. It was a mammoth gathering of three Naga tribes; the Yimchungers, the Sangtams and the Eastern Sümis. The meeting deliberated on the grave situation that had surfaced in the region and the urgent need for armed retaliation against the Indian troops was debated. It was concluded with a collective resolution to resist the Indian forces. Further, the three tribes unanimously agreed that Kaito Sukhai, the leader of Naga Safe Guard, head the armed movement, as acting General. The following leaders were also chosen to strengthen the Naga Safe Guard army; Niheto of Aquba, Viniho of Khekiye, Samphu Yimchunger and Pomba Yimchunger. It was also suggested that General Kaito Sukhai might induct some top rank and file at his discretion. Within a few months, General Kaito appointed the following officers to his fold: Lovihe of Lukhuyi, Simon Pukhato of Sichimi, Zheluto of Ghukhuyi, Khughoto of Hoshepu, Khezheto of Nihoshe, Hozheto of Hoshepu, Khughozu of Khewoto, Pukiye of Thokihi, and Mithizu of Hutami.

Subsequently, with the consent of the village chiefs of Khekiye, Hoshepu, Nihoshe and Khewoto of Aghushito, Kaito was allowed to set up his garrison headquarter in the region. The four villages, jointly known as 'Aghushito' meaning 'Hills of battle', were established by Kaito's ancestors not long before. For instance, Nihoshe village was established just about 30 years previously, by General Kaito's uncles, Nihoshe and Vikihe Zhimomi.

What followed, after the raising of a battle fort at Hoshepu, was a massive recruitment drive of volunteers into the Naga Safe Guards army. Within months of the historic meeting, Naga Safe Guards began to sketch out an ingenious war plan to engage in combat against the mammoth Indian forces. Kaito planned to experiment, during the first armed combat, by utilizing the tactics of fortress battle. Preparation for battle, at Hoshepu valley, included digging defence lines and trenches at different rendezvous and strategic locations.

The main defence line was set at Khewoto village, which was located to the north of Hoshepu village. A trench 6 feet deep, 8 feet wide, and 220 yards long was dug with the help of villagers. The villagers willingly gave their voluntary services, and also provided all materials required by the Naga Safe Guards. By May 1955, an extensive thick defence line was built out of huge alder-tree trunks stacked in four layers. The surround was covered by thousands of deadly seasonal bamboo spikes. Khekiye village, close to Hoshepu, was made the General Headquarters, where the chief of Naga Safe Guards camped. While the strategic posts spread over Nihoshe village, in the south of Hoshepu, which served as the defence outpost, Hoshepu village, located between Khekiye and Khewoto, served as the communication centre between the Headquarters and the key defence line at Khewoto, where the battle took place.

The news was soon dispatched to the Assam Rifles about a surge in Naga army camps in the Hoshepu area. All wary eyes were focused on the area most occupied by Naga fighters. Government forces resolved to wipe out the garrison at Hoshepu, as they anticipated ever bigger revolts. When the Assistant Indian Political Officer of Aghunato, S.D. Lakhar sent out the army, in undersized column, to attack the Naga army camps, the latter seized the opportunity to sabotage the rival with ease. Kaito's men started considering the Assam Rifles as their feeble foes. With little difficulty, they outmanoeuvred them, snatching away guns and bullets, at every opportunity, and thus, filling up their armoury for further exploits.

According to Ikishe Sukhalu, one of the loyal soldiers of General Kaito and the person in charge of maintaining records of arms and ammunitions, captured from enemies, the Naga Safe Guards seized around 16 Indian-army guns and a great deal of ammunitions, prior to the battle of Hoshepu. The huge yield for the Naga Safe Guards was receiving an immense support from the villagers of Aghushito in terms of manpower, weaponry, food and other essential items. The villagers of Aghushito, mostly the energetic youths, would also voluntarily act as spies. They disclosed every detail of the Indian Army movement, such as the direction in which they are coming, going and also the number of cadres and the company or regiment to which they belonged. Their participation not only enhanced the morale of the Naga Safe Guards, but also the information they provided was vital for General Kaito, while strategizing his manoeuvres, especially for the ambush tactics. The dividends of such operations were indicated in the encounters which took place at a number of villages like Ngozubo, Aquba, Thokihi, Tokiye, Viyixe and Viyilho. Despite several increasing assaults, from the beginning of May to September 3rd 1955, by the Assam Rifles, they still failed to penetrate the fortified camp at Khewoto village. It was only on 4th September that the Indian Armed Force, with reinforcements, could close in around the fortified zone and engage in one of the fiercest battles ever fought in Naga history, known as the battle of Hoshepu or the First Indo-Naga battle.

Indeed, it was a very unassuming beginning. Other than the General's personally purchased guns, and a few donated by the villagers, they had to start from scratch with scarce weapons, and without a strong logistic footing at their disposal. Nevertheless, under the sharp supervision of this bright young leader, Naga fighters started progressing in many ways: they built up their armouries by frequently seizing the weapons of the Indian army, after surprise attacks and ambushes. The Indian Army often engaged village labourers, in groups of a hundred or more, to transport heavy loads of bullets and grenades. At times, the labourers escaped with their stacks and brought them to the Naga Safe Guards camp at Hoshepu, instead of delivering to the designated Indian Army camp. The brave acts of the villagers presented a great opportunity to the Naga Army. The ingenuity of General Kaito was proven by the manner in which he masterminded the capture of arms and ammunitions, without directly engaging the enemy. It also served the purpose of preserving the precious lives of his soldiers. Sometimes, he would send his soldiers, disguised as coolies, along with the villagers to carry loads for the India Army. The plan worked out perfectly, with the seizure of the much-required arms and ammunitions. Vikuho Zhimomi, one of Kaito's faithful soldier, and also his personal bodyguard, remembers being sent on one such successful mission, braving the possible consequences. Vikuho recalls bringing back his booty, which contained twelve grenades and two hundred bullets. Vikuho Zhimomi also relates how he surrendered himself to the Indian-groomed Village Guards under the instruction of his superior Kaito. The Village-Guards personnel were happy when Kaito's most loyal soldier had surrendered to them, but their happiness was short-lived, when, on 9 September, 1959, they learned that Vikuho had emptied their arms store, and decamped with 33 rifles, 3,000 rounds, 2,000 rupees and 11 Village-Guards personnel to General Kaito's camp. In another incident, Kaito along with Ikishe Sukhalu, at the former's insistence, dug up the WWII used arms and ammunitions that Ikishe's father, Hutoi Sukhalu, had buried in his room. They took possession of 5 Japanese rifles, 1 LMG and 3,000 rounds of bullets.

Vikuho Zhimomi (now 89 years old), former General Kaito's personal bodyguard and one of the first batch of the Naga Army also the only participant in the first Indo-Naga battle still living.

The limited weapons were tactfully utilized under the strict instruction of General Kaito. He issued one gun with five bullets to three soldiers; the best shooter among the three was to hold the gun. Whenever an Indian soldier was shot down or wounded, it was the task of the second soldier to snatch away the enemy's gun. The third soldier, armed with machete, would jump in and collect the bullet strips strapped around the waist of the dead enemy, which generally contained 50 bullets. They were under strict orders to fire only when their targets were certain. The most challenging task was that out of the five bullets issued, three bullets should kill three enemies; one bullet was to be fired when they were about to be captured; and the last bullet was to be reserved for guarding the assigned gun. Fascinatingly, General Kaito even challenged his soldiers to kill two enemies with a single bullet – a feat he had achieved often. Because of this, Naga fighters became a deadly threat to the Indian soldiers.

One of the key hurdles, during the preparation of this battle, was the lack of adequate training for the Naga soldiers. The soldiers consisted mostly of young villagers with no prior exposure to warfare skills. The presence of Indian-trained soldiers of the calibre of Major Simon Pukhato in the NSG fraternity had a great influence on General Kaito's new recruits. Major Simon Pukhato had served in the Assam Rifles regiment for fourteen years and had to serve just one more year to be able to claim his pension benefits but he even relinquished his pension to serve the Nagas. The killing, torture, humiliation and prejudices meted out to his Naga brethren by the Indian soldiers constrained him to join the Naga Safe Guards. On 16 June, 1955, he even recalls the time, it was 3:30 p.m., when he surrendered his service rifle with 350 bullets to General Kaito and was appointed in the rank of Major. The General was so elated; he even christened his new recruit 'Pukhato' which means: 'The one who saves and protects his people'. People started addressing him as 'Simon Pukhato'. His earlier training and years of experience at the Assam Regiment made him the most qualified person to train the inexperienced Naga soldiers. General Kaito assigned him to train the soldiers in all the basic skills, like handling guns, and how to take up position when the enemy attacks. Pukhato trained them for a month or so.

At this stage, the Naga Safe Guards could be construed as a sort of militia because the fact was that the forces were raised, more or less, from a few loyalists and peasants. There was a funny incident where an elderly Naga soldier had been taught to salute superior officers. Coming to report about his mission, at their camp one day, he saw two officers standing. One was none other than General Kaito Sukhai, and the other was his elder brother Kughato Sukhai, the Prime Minister. The soldier came to attention and stamping his feet as hard as possible saluted them by raising both his hands simultaneously to his forehead. When reprimanded by the General that it was not the proper way to salute, he replied: "But there are two of you there, so I thought I should raise both hands". Whatever their shortcomings were, they were the ones who had come together voluntarily to fight for the cause of their self-determination. They reckoned that the call to reclaim Naga sovereignty was real and urgent, and even though many did not know the basic method of modern warfare, they never wavered their intent to ward-off the enemy. Shortage of weapons was another barrier, yet they stood their ground and made supreme efforts. After the completion of their training, the eleven soldiers along with Major Simon Pukhato were sent to the main defence line at Khewoto camp.

On July 17, 1955, an ambush on the Assam Rifles was carefully executed by the Naga soldiers, near Tokiye town school grounds, under the direction of their chief Kaito Sukhai. Major Simon Pukhato, the Commanding Officer, for this operation, shot to death the entire thirteen Indian soldiers. After that, a series of ambushes followed. The news of intense attacks had alarmed New Delhi which left them with no choice but to unleash a pack of wild legions, the 17th Indian Rajputs, to Hoshepu range. On 24 August, Naga fighters got a tip-off that a brigade of the Indian Army would be arriving to assist the Assam Rifles. Indeed, after that, Indian Army surveillance, around Hoshepu, was frequent. The Naga Safe Guards, sensing that the rapid movement of the rival forces demanded a more careful movement, paid more attention to their routine raids. Thus, the bell began to toll, calling out for the final battle preparation. A mixed sense of thrill and anxiety filled the air, in both camps as the inevitable baptism of battle between the two equipped groups fast approached.

On 4 September, the combined forces of the 17th Indian Rajputs and the Assam Rifles were deployed to flush out the Naga fighters. Nagas were on one side of the hillock while the Indian forces were on the other, with a distance between them of just around 150 feet. An exchange of gun fire was delayed, as they initially engaged in war of words, exchanging insults and provocations.

Indian soldiers shouted:

> "Why are you Nagas very proud of yourselves? Do you have anything of which you can be proud? Your days are numbered. We are going to finish you, soon. We don't have to use our guns. We will catch you alive with our bare hands and kill you."

The verbal challenge of the Naga soldiers was a ploy to provoke the Indian army to chase them towards the deadly bamboo snares which were fenced in thousands around the fortified post. Major Pukhato commanded his soldiers to walk around bare-handed, in a provocative manner, and sure enough the Indian Major fell for the bait. He ordered his soldiers to leave their guns and chase the unarmed Nagas. Around fifty to sixty Indian soldiers who came charging toward the Nagas were impaled and most were killed as they fell into the pit of razor-sharp bamboo spike traps set by the Nagas. More were gunned down by the Naga fighters, as they hurried in, to take back the injured and dead fellow soldiers. This caught the enemy by surprise.

Besides the bamboo spike traps, another inventive plan of Kaito was tying a rope to tree branches with a concealed guerrilla holding the other end of the rope. When the ever-prepared rival lurked in, the agile Naga would pull the string and shake the trees, which caused the rival column to exhaust their entire shots into the indistinct area. Simultaneously, the well positioned Naga fighters would appear out of the blue, lob their grenades and shell their rounds into the line of puzzled enemies.

Another round of verbal confrontation began.

Naga soldiers: "We are not afraid of you. We are fighting for our freedom and our sovereignty. Come, look at us! We are without our guns, come and catch us."

Indian soldier: "Why are you so proud? We are going to peel-off your skin and make you suffer."

Indian Major (in Hindi): "Hum log ek brigade hai. Aap sirf bara admi kya karoge? (What can you twelve soldiers do when we have the entire brigade on our side?)"

Major Pukhato: "Oh, Major Sahib! Even if you keep on talking, one bullet is enough to kill you. Do you know that you are speaking your last words? There are not many of us here, but I have twelve Sümi warriors with me. Twelve of us are at par with twelve hundred soldiers and twelve soldiers are enough to finish off your brigade."

Indian Major: "How dare you utter such gross words? What power do you have? Do you think you are invincible?"

Major Pukhato: "We come in the name of the Lord Jesus Christ who has given us the power to crush you and your soldiers. You can say whatever you want but those will be your last words."

Indian Major: "What can a mere Sümi bullet do? It cannot kill anyone."

The pride of the Indian Major infuriated Pukhato. He took out his gun, aimed carefully at the Major and fired at him; the shot killed him instantly on the spot. Pukhato commanded his soldiers to start firing at the Indian Soldiers. The villagers were right behind them. He ordered the villagers to leave the battle site immediately and seek for safety, lest they get killed or injured. A heavy gun battle followed. And thus began the battle of Hoshepu.

The fierce firing on both fronts continued. Naga soldiers took turns to sleep and fired their guns right from dusk to dawn. Any possibility of the enemy encroaching was prevented by vigilant sharpshooters. The role of the women folk of Khewoto village was yet another integral part of this battle: Braving the bullets, they literally crawled towards the bunker where the Naga soldier were positioned, carrying with them the pre-mixed rice and pork curry on a wooden plate; they handfed their soldiers who were busy engaged in firing at the rivals. The women were paired in twos, one for carrying food and the other for water. The soldiers were routinely fed twice a day. The battle pursued, but a setback occurred on the fifth day. On September 8, around 8 p.m., Major Pukhato was gravely wounded as a result of the burst of a three-inch mortar, and immediately left the battle field. Another soldier, Honito of Hoshepu, was badly injured too.

The Indian Army constantly dropped bombs and poured volleys of shells into the Naga Army camp. By September 10, five Naga patriots; Vitomo of Lithsami, Jehoto of Kulhopu, Ahoto of Hoshepu, Vighoto of Hoshepu, and Viniqhe of Khekiye had been killed. The Nagas arrived to a point where they could no longer equal their superior rival. They seemed to have exhausted their entire wit to confront the enemy. They ran short of manpower and ammunition. Taking advantage of the situation, the Indian Army closed in from different directions. After seven days of fierce fighting, braving all odds, the Nagas finally surrendered their fortified post at Khewoto and started deserting their other strongholds too. The Indian soldiers had occupied the main post, by at 11:30 a.m. on the same day.

The entire village of Aghushito as well as the Naga forces posted in this valley had to flee for safety on the night of September 9. Some could escape only at dawn. The strategy of the Indian Rajputs and the Assam Rifles, to enfold the Naga fighters from different directions, backfired on them. They ended up shelling among themselves. It was total chaos and confusion, the Indian Rajputs mistook the Assam Rifles as Naga fighters, and began firing at them, while the Assam Rifles countered by striking back at the Indian Rajputs. It was sheer lunacy on the part of the Indian forces and the blunder of the cross firing took a huge toll on Indian soldiers.

After decamping Hoshepu, the Naga fighters went to Ghukhuyi, the native village of their commander General Kaito. At the village, the fighters were welcomed with a grand reception. A big Sümi feast of rice, pork and beef deemed fit for Naga warriors was served to the weary fighters. They stayed at Ghukhuyi for few months and then moved on to Xuivi village, which became their Headquarters for some time. The aftermath of the battle was mass destruction of the villages of the Hoshepu area. Houses and granaries were razed; and the entire population of the area had to flee for safety to neighbouring villages. The reality of their displacement from their birthplace caused emotional wounds. The burning down of granaries and houses left them economically insecure; and the Indian military surveillance deprived them of their free movement. They faced the bitterest ravages of the war – they were angered, saddened and confused; and they had to bore pain, misery and perplexity, all at once.

Kaito and his fighters were well aware of their fragile position in terms of their limited sources of weapons. However, the unusual, jagged, and tricky terrain worked to their ideal advantage. In reality, the Indian Army was fully funded and equipped by the Central Government, with a mission to flush out the Naga insurgency; but, for the Naga fighters, it was endurance and courage that sustained them throughout the ordeal. What emerged from this struggle and hardship, and the inevitable face off with the far-superior foe, was an eventual recognition that the Nagas were now on a par with one of the mightiest militaries in the world. A huge price was paid in terms of shedding the precious blood and life of many soldiers on both sides. However, this terrifying ground reality of bloody and violent combat brought to light their zest, their zeal and their courage, and also re-affirmed their pledge to liberate their homeland from foreign hands. The battle of Hoshepu, the first and the fiercest battle ever waged or fought with the Indian Army on Naga soil, would historically remain an important landmark in the entire narration of the Naga freedom movement.

In Kaito's own assessment of the battle of Hoshepu, he realized that the fortress tactics tried by the Naga army had proved to be an expensive and impractical strategy. So, thereafter, he decided to shift his tactics to guerrilla warfare, which was more suitable to local terrain and also would be less challenging for his limited fighting force. The Indian Army took cognizance of these tribal warriors as formidable foes, whose deadly combination of unrelenting spirit and thirst to fight against their enemy should not be taken as sheer pretence or reckoned as the work of mere spontaneous radicals. After the war, General Kaito proclaimed:

> "The roaring blast of Indian Army bombs took the lives of five Naga soldiers, but the gust of Naga courage had slain hundreds of Indian personnel. Indian casualty reports will continue to increase as we have the courage and the terrain to our gain."

Incredibly, with just a cluster of 16 soldiers and support of the village volunteers, General Kaito brought down about 380 enemies (as per the record on the First Indo-Naga battle Jubilee souvenir) at the cost of 5 brave souls, and though the Nagas had lost the battle they didn't lose the war.

Late Khezheto Awomi of Nihoshe village, former Captain of the first batch of the Naga Army and the participants of the first Indo-Naga battle.

Four

The bracing of Naga Armed Forces

It was the dawn of spring 1956, when the Naga National Council (NNC) launched the Federal Government of Nagaland (FGN) with the endorsement of Naga people. This development, however, was totally negated by the government of India. Nevertheless, the FGN was formally declared on 22 March, 1956 and unfurled their Flag at Phenshunyu, Rengma Naga village, some 40 kilometres away from the State capital, Kohima. The objective was to maintain all the features of a democratic pattern of government, headed by the Prime Minister, and fifteen cabinet Ministers. Also, on 22 March, 1956, Kaito Sukhai the founder and acting General of the Naga Safe Guards army was officially appointed as the Commander-in-Chief of the Federal Government Army.

SPLIT IN NAGA REBEL RANKS

COUNCIL DISSOLVED
FROM OUR OWN CORRESPONDENT
DELHI, MAY 14

Zapu Phizo, the rebel Naga leader, has dissolved the Naga national council, of which he is president, and placed its vice-president, Ingkomeren, under house arrest, according to the Indian news agency reports from Shillong. Ingkomeren is stated to have headed a group of moderates opposed to the "murderous methods of campaign" pursued by Phizo and his supporters. After the dissolution of the council, Phizo is reported to have proclaimed conscription in Naga villages, and to have appointed a leader named Kaito as "commander-in-chief of the Naga homeland army."

Reports of a split in the rebel camp are welcomed by the Indian Press as the first sign of a weakening of the Naga front, but the immediate results seem likely to be an intensification of the struggle. Encounters between uniformed rebels and Indian troops, and acts of sabotage on roads and bridges, continue to be reported almost daily.

Indian Newspaper reports on the appointment of Kaito as Commander-in-Chief of Naga Army, May 14, 1956.

Six months had passed since the battle of Hoshepu; the infliction of brutality upon the Nagas was growing by days. Innocent communities, especially the relatives of the Naga fighters, the sympathizers, and village elders were taken into custody and were grilled and charged with abetting the Naga army. Some died in confinement, while the fortunate ones came back with damaged limbs, broken ribs or swollen eyes; and in the worst cases, even their skins peeled. Nehru's fury was unleashed upon the Nagas.

Before the influx of Indian forces such brutal acts were rare in the Naga domain. The sanctity of Naga people's mores and customs had been breached in the most brazen manner. Anguished and humiliated, agonized, emotionally and physically, their tolerance level had been surpassed. However, these innocent civilians could do little, other than submit their grievances to General Kaito and his followers. Among the scores of such brutal companies, placed in the hills, to suppress the Naga people were the infamous Assam Border Police, stationed at British Inspection Bungalow, near Satakha village, since 1954. Subedar Hazarika was the Commander of this villainous company. In early March, 1956, one Naga Safe Guard volunteer, Natohe Muru of Vishepu village, was captured by Subedar Hazarika and his company. They splintered all his bones. Natohe died as a result of this torture. Later, the Assam Police claimed that Natohe was killed because he tried to escape. This was a cover up. When they heard of Natohe's agonizing death, General Kaito and his followers were infuriated and grief-stricken. On receiving the news, Kaito reacted with a derisive smile, which was ominous. He was burning to avenge Natohe's death, but while devising a suitable plan, he refrained from taking impulsive steps.

During the following days, Kaito silently planned to deliver a lesson to that pitiless company. He gathered together a substantial number of crudely trained men, and an ample quantity of old weapon supplies which had been used in the previous battle. A bitter but heroic taste of war, with a far greater force, at the Battle of Hoshepu, had given him an understanding of fighting. This time he ought to be more astute. He would be marching into an enemy's established territory and the modus operandi would have to be different unlike the preceding battle. Kaito had lost five soldiers in the previous battle, this time he would not lose one. That would be the priority. Further, the motive of this attack wasn't just revenge. It would be an attempt to stimulate the fervour of the young to join his arms movement that had already been established.

The British Inspection Bungalow happened to be located few miles away from the Naga Safe Guard Headquarters, in Xuivi. General Kaito called three of his men, Lt. Colonel Yeveto, Major Viniho, and Captain Khughoto to Xuivi village, and laid out his plan. Soon after, he secretly went to meet Scato Swu who was then the Headmaster of Satakha, High school. Scato Swu was the third graduate among his tribesman and would later become the President of FGN, and few years subsequent to this event he married Hotoli Swu, the elder sister of General Kaito.

General Kaito asked for Scato to send some of his students to survey inside the Assam police camp. The latter sent five of his active students to Kaito. He was using the students to avoid any suspicion. The plan was to let these students sneak into the police camp and locate the wireless transmitter. After locating the transmitter, they were to mark the site with chalk from outside without arousing the suspicions of others. Kaito wished to destroy the radio transmitter, so that when the attack ensued, the inmates would be left without means of communication. Five students Vihoje, Ghonito, Zhehuto, Yezheto and L. Atoi Swu were sent to execute this task. They did their job flawlessly, as instructed, and reported back to Kaito.

Before proceeding, Kaito had a meeting with the volunteers from the adjoining villages, and informed them of his plan, to attack the Satakha police post. The volunteers were told to assist the Naga Safe Guard personnel with food supplies and other essential needs as the battle might be prolonged. On 23 March, 1956, Gen. Kaito sent informants to advise the NSGS personnel stationed at various locations to gather at Satakha. He fixed the timing of the attack at noon, to which one of his officers Vishito responded:

"It is impractical to attack during daylight, why don't we take them out at night"

The General answered: "Ache[3], at noon the Assam Police personnel will be resting, after their lunch, and most of them will be sleeping without guns. We shall surprise them while they are drowsy. Now go and inform all the Naga Safe Guards personnel and volunteers."

Vishito agreed and went about with the task.

On March 24, 1956, precisely at 11:30 a.m., 38 personnel of NSG, under the direct command of General Kaito Sukhai, arrived at the appointed site. Everyone took their position and slouched down secured, and watched the entire movement at the police camp down below. As directed, all eyes were perched on the primary objective, which was the radio transmitter. Nagas had surrounded the camp from all directions; even the gutsy volunteers were set to swoop down with machetes and spears. Exactly at the stroke of noon, a stream of bullets was showered upon the marked position of the radio transmitter, eventually dismantling it. A brief silence and then hundreds of voices in unison began to howl a symbolic Naga war cry "Au….he…he…he…he…!", followed by volunteers pounding empty tin drums from different directions. The foreboding clamours, accompanied by sounds of rattling gunfire, emitting from every corner, sent tremors into the police camp. The Assam police were caught off guard and they ran helter-skelter.

One of Kaito's favourite tactics was to play a war of nerves with the enemy. Before attacking, he would foment fears in enemy's morale, and while they were unsettled, he would boldly take advantage, and

---

3 'Ache' was a pet name for Vishoto.

overpower them. If only his enemies had known of his vulnerable position in terms of manpower and weapons, they would have been utterly surprised. Kaito's first plan was to dismantle the radio and then play with the enemy's psyche by creating panic. The plan went perfectly well, as there was no concern over enemy's reinforcement, since the communication line had been snapped, and even the water supply was severed. Naga fighters had sufficient time, before launching the attack, and had, by then, occupied every vantage position. The slightest, miscalculated movement, inside the police camp might provoke fatal shots.

It was 4 p.m., and the exchange of gunfire continued. General Kaito beckoned Lt. Col. Yeveto and told him to parley with the besieged Assam Police personnel. Lt. Col. Yeveto Zhimomi, before joining the Naga Safe Guards, had served in the Assam Regiment and could speak fluent Hindi. Kaito instructed Yeveto to tell the Assam police that the Nagas would kill everyone inside the camp, if they did not surrender. As instructed, Yeveto, at the top of his voice, started to shout in Hindi: "Surrender peacefully or else we will kill everyone". Again, he shouted: "The Indian Police post, at Zunheboto, has been captured, and Indian police, from Kilomi and Dzulhami, have also surrendered to us. Therefore, as no one is coming to help you, so you better surrender."

To which Indian police commander Subedar Hazarika, yelled back: "Stop firing, we are willing to surrender." Hazirika insisted that the invading party should come down to the camp and negotiate. The Naga fighters, on the other hand were not willing to go inside. They insisted that the besieged personnel should come out, with their hands raised above their heads. The exchange of words as to who should come towards whom went on until, Gen. Kaito opined that the commanders of the opposing parties should come and meet at the gate of the camp. This suggestion was agreed and was promptly carried out.

Lt. Col. Yeveto, representing the Naga Army, proudly progressed towards the gate, while Indian police commander Hazarika came out and met him at the gate. It was an unusual sight to see the two opposing commanders shaking hands gracefully, subsequent to the fierce gun battle. Yeveto laid out the conditions to the Indian commander, that his men should lay down their arms and surrender peacefully, so as to avoid further bloodshed. In return, the police personnel would be given safe custody, and set free, unharmed. Thus, the Indian police agreed to the terms and surrendered without further argument. The Nagas could not recollect any event, where such a humane deal was offered to them, by the Indian Armed forces. They ended the day by capturing 78 police personnel with an assortment of 77 weapons, a large stock of ammunition, and one damaged LMG. This was, possibly, the largest amount of ammunition seized from the enemy, up to that time.

Surrendered personnel were taken, on foot, to makeshift FGN headquarters, at Xuivi village, which was around five kilometres from Satakha. Next day, 25 March 1956, Scato Swu, Kughato Sukhai and Zuheto Swu interrogated the prisoners. After a lengthy consideration, the Federal Government of Nagaland resolved to set free the captives, without any pre-conditions, but with a keen expectation, that the government of India would reciprocate, by letting free those Nagas languishing in Indian Jails. But in the end, the kind gesture shown towards the captives proved unfruitful. A letter, addressed to the Government of India, was handed over to these captives to be delivered to the Indian authorities. The letter was drafted and written by Scato Swu and the same is being recorded below;

The letter reads:

Memo No. EIP/4/1, 27-3-1956.

The Government of India is torturing the whole population of Nagaland, regardless of innocence or guilt. It is, however, never the policy of Federal Government of Nagaland to commit any inhuman deed towards Indian captives that may fall within the powers of Federal Government of Nagaland. We, the Nagas are very conscious that both Nagas and Indians are human beings, and therefore, it is not for the Federal Government of Nagaland to torture or kill Indian brothers. Therefore, they let the 78 Indian captives go their own way home, as God created them free people. It is hoped that a good number of Nagas, now in Indian jails may kindly be freed, too.

As the captives had to cross different regions / areas to reach Kohima, a letter of safety was written in three different languages, and handed to them. The same are being reproduced here below:

Letter written in English version:

These captives are being set free by the Federal Government of Nagaland. Nobody will harass them or inflict them in any manner. Take care of them till they reach Kohima.

Letter written in Angami version:

Kedima hako Federal Government of Nagaland bu uko phrishu wazia. Miapuo rei hako pechu-penyuile kenju. Uko tuovo kewhima tsokemochie khruhi shulie#.

Letter written in Sümi version:

Akughumi hipaqo ye Federal Government of Nagaland no phevetsu ani. Khumu panongu pishi-puju momu ghime mla. Kohima to miphi lo akivi shi panongu julo.

In the annals of the Indo-Naga armed conflicts, the seizure of weapons at Satakha was the largest ever by the Naga Army. It provided a basis for the otherwise almost empty arsenal of the Naga Army. On the other hand, this event had the Assam police disgraced and grounded. It also presented a humiliating picture of the entire Indian forces.

The capture was a further spur to the progress of the Naga freedom movement. News of their powerful victory spread like wildfire. It aroused patriotism within the young bloods. They were thrilled and taken by the accounts of a daring young general, under whose command the enemy had been squatted and disgraced. Thereafter, the Naga Army began swelling in numbers, as youths began to leave their schools, colleges and their daily jobs, to enrol into the fold and fight for a noble cause.

To prevent humiliation, the attack of Satakha Assam Police Camp was reported, by Assam Chief Minister Bisnuram Medhi, as "abandoned by the Assam police". The reality is that it was attacked and captured, rather cleverly, with no loss of lives or injury sustained by the Naga Army.

Three months after General Kaito captured Satakha Assam Police Camp, Phizo along with Thungti Chang similarly planned an attack on Kohima Garrison. The strike began on 4 June, 1956. The attacking, however, did not go well, as planned. They send a messenger to General Kaito's Naga Army headquarters at Old Shena village with a request for urgent reinforcements. Lt. Colonel J.P. Vikugha, one of Kaito's nimble officers, was there when the messenger arrived and Vikugha informed the messenger that their Commander-in-Chief was enraged because the attack on Kohima Garrison had been launched with no proper grounding. But reluctant to see his Naga fighters beaten down, Kaito decided to send his fighters to capture the Kohima Garrison alongside Phizo's and Thungti's fighters. He sent troops to Kohima under the command of another of his skilled officers, Lieutenant Colonel Vikuho Tuccu.

It has been narrated by some, that Kaito withdrew his fighters from Kohima when he learnt that Phizo was still going to favour Thungti over him as the Commander-in-Chief, despite Kaito having been officially appointed by the Federal Government of Nagaland, on 22 March, 1956, three months prior to that incident. But that was a half-truth. Right from the beginning, General Kaito knew that Phizo did not favour his armed leadership. Therefore, if that were the sole reason for Kaito's fighters' withdrawal, he would have not dispatched them to Kohima in the first place.

It took little more than a day for Lieutenant Colonel Vikuho Tuccu and his troops to travel, on foot, from Old Shena to Kohima. Coming from the direction of the small WWII airstrip, which was then located at the current Nagaland New Secretariat Complex, they arrived at Kohima village. After some days of fighting, Kaito's fighters swiftly advanced and finally captured the entire civilian area, in and around the south of Assam Rifles Garrison, and were set to attack the main base. But it appeared that there was no advancement from the north of the garrison, where Thungti and his fighters had earlier agreed to charge in, so Kaito's fighters, after a careful calculation, decided to retreat. After Kaito's fighters withdrew, Thungti could not progress the attack, and eventually the siege of Kohima failed.

B.N. Mullick, an advisor to Nehru stated in his book My Years with Nehru (1948-1964)

> *Kaito, with his entire Sema force, withdrew from Kohima, making it easy for the Indian Army and the Assam Rifles to clear the weakened Naga forces, under Thungti Chang, from the Naga village. For the three days Kohima remained cut off from India and the greater part of the village remained under Phizo's control.*

He further commented...

Had Kaito's leadership of the Naga armed forces been recognised and appreciated, the capture of Kohima could have succeeded.

History may perhaps have been scripted differently on this account, too.

Five

The cost of freedom

Brene Brown shared on her TED Talks a powerful statement: "You can choose courage, or you can choose comfort, but you cannot choose both!"

Even as the world slept serenely, the Nagas were reeling under the weight of tyranny. The Indian forces fiddled the tune of oppression while Nagas feebly defended themselves from the iron fists of Nehru's India to safeguard their sovereign rights. Massive manhunts for the Naga freedom fighters had surged. Each day and night, central militaries and Assam police randomly apprehended the alleged Naga national workers, the innocent families and sympathizers of the national movement. They were detained and afterwards tortured. Ignominy was at its best - women were raped, churches debased, village chiefs disgraced, even killed on some counts, while their mutilated bodies were displayed in public places for people to witness the horrific sight and thereby quench the fervour for freedom in their minds. The elders, who survived those tragic years live to tell the tales.

The year was 1956, and General Kaito Sukhai's siblings —younger sister Vitoli, a gorgeous girl with a pleasant smile and demure features, and younger brother Phoishe, a lanky teenage boy with facial resemblance to his older brother Kaito, were studying at Mission School Kohima. Coming from a family who had been unconditionally supporting the Naga National Movement, they could understand the fact that the

Nagas have every right to be an independent Nation, and felt that the war their family had been shouldering was not a worthless fight. Seeing that their two elder brothers, Kughato and Kaito Sukhai, were spearheading the movement, these younger siblings could well suppose that their fair share of troubles would soon land on their doorstep. There was nothing they could do but anticipate the day with fear.

As expected, one fateful day in the month of October 1956, visitors, clad in khaki regulars, came barging into their rented home at Kohima and forcibly took away Phoishe, the younger of the two siblings. Those days, be it in Kohima or any other area within the Naga hills, it wasn't an odd occurrence, to be visited by the uniformed personnel and they were therefore un-surprised by the visit. However, at the particular time, they were least prepared for such event for they had no close-family members nor any close associates to relay their trouble, if any untoward incident happened. The sole purpose of the siblings staying at Kohima was for schooling. Their native home was at Ghukhuyi village in Zunheboto, about 140 kilometres away from Kohima town.

They were wholly unaware that both their parents were languishing in prison. Their father Kuhoto was being held in Jorhat jail for providing shelter and food for the Naga freedom fighters. Prior to this sentence Kuhoto had been arrested a whopping 24 times by the Indian police, for abetting his fellow Naga fighters. Their mother Kiholi had been confined at Zhekiye village Army concentration camp for the same reason. Their eldest sister Hotoli had taken Kuhoi, the youngest brother and gone into underground hiding, while the two eldest brothers, Kughato and Kaito, were spearheading the rebellion. Gen. Kaito was on the rampage, striking terror wherever he went, and inciting panic in the minds of Indian troops. He had created a massive uproar at the Indian government desk. At the same time, Kaito had brought upon his family, great burdens as the price of Naga national movement. The Indian Intelligence was totally focused on apprehending this young leader.

Vitoli was in tears and wondering who could help her. She didn't know anyone to whom she could turn. She was the sole guardian of Phoishe and it would not be possible for her to continue living, if something awful should happen to him. She was fearful that maybe worse could be done to Phoishe. Perhaps, they might even kill him while torturing him. In those days, if someone were whisked away by uniformed personnel, the person could end up being murdered regardless of whether he or she knew something or nothing about the affairs of the Movement. Phoishe, a 13-year-old child, was confined in Kohima prison for the sole reason of being the brother of Kaito and Kughato Sukhai.

Vitoli gathered her wits. She thought she ought to release her brother by whatever means were available. One of her friend's, named Ruth Angami, accompanied her to the police station and met a police officer named Keyakire. By good fortune, the officer happens to be an Angami Naga. She pleaded with the Naga officer to release the boy who was just an innocent juvenile student. The officer listened to her intently and with perceptible compassion, and although willing to help, regretfully asserted that releasing Phoishe was not within his power, as Phoishe had already been labelled a political prisoner.

Saddened and confused, Vitoli could neither bail out her brother nor return to her already abandoned house, in the village, as it had been burnt down by the Indian Army, as many as three times. And it was evident that this time too her house had been razed to ashes. Their belongings, granaries and the stocks had been scorched to ground by the Indian armed forces. If she stayed back at Kohima, she could be facing the same fate of her brother, and it was known that the plight of female prisoners was no better than that of a male detainee and often worse. Even her brother, Phoishe had advised her to leave Kohima to seek her third brother, Vikuto, as he could take care of himself. On her last visit to him, with tears welled up in her eyes, she bade adieu to Phoishe. Her solace then rested with faith alone. She prayed for her and her family's safekeeping, and then decided to seek her brother, Vikuto, who was then studying at Government High School Shillong.

Vitoli had never been to Shillong. Those days, there were no phones and the only mode of communication was telegram. At first her innocent mind could not even comprehend how telegrams were sent, until her friend, Ruth Angami, helped her to write a letter to her brother about the troubles that had befallen her and her family, back in Nagaland, and explaining that she had no choice other than to come to Shillong and stay with him. Fortunately, for Vitoli, Vikuto responded back, within a week, and told her to come to Shillong, as soon as she could.

As a young girl it was a terrifying decision. The journey she was going to embark on was extremely strange, somewhat exhilarating too. Never before in her life had she ventured on a lengthy trip other than to Kohima town. She packed a few belongings, took out the ninety rupees which her mother had given her, when sending her off to Kohima and, full of courage and faith in God, she left on a truck bound for Dimapur, since there were no buses, back then. With few clumps of scattered human dwellers otherwise Dimapur was just a vast expanse of dense forest infested with dacoits (armed robbers) and wild elephants. The only good thing was that the railway line, in Dimapur, was in operation, ever since the advent of British. Thus, from there, she boarded a train to Guwahati, and from Guwahati she was picked by her cousin Kiyekhu who was sent by Vikuto.

Even after reaching her brother's place at Shillong, every now and then, her concerns reverted back to family. Her entire family had been scattered and it was unknown, if they were even alive. Even if they were, she couldn't find the means to bring them together. There seemed to be nothing she could do.

That following month, at Vikuto's persistence, Vitoli was admitted into the prestigious Pine Mount School, in Shillong, and started attending a normal school. Everything about Shillong was beautiful and serene: pleasant weather conditions, splendid landscapes, and fine-looking Khasi and Garo people dressed in multi-coloured attires added vibrancy to this magnificent hill station. Apart from the grim political situation in the Naga Hills, Nagaland in many respects is identical to Meghalaya, but karma for Vitoli at Shillong couldn't last.

Late one afternoon, while returning home, after school, Vitoli encountered a Naga lady, named Mrs Zhevili Lukheyi Sema, who was well-known to her. The lady was probably returning home, after shopping. The unusual thing was that the lady didn't even raise her eyes, as they passed each other. She appeared to be evading Vitoli. What could be the problem? As Vitoli was about to pass by, the lady, without meeting her eyes, uttered in a rather muffled tone, 'Anga' (child), you are being pursued by 'the men in boots', meaning the police. Vitoli understood well what the lady was trying to convey. Her naïve mind was thinking rapidly, could it be possible, the Assam police from Kohima had followed her to Shillong? At that instant the uniformed personnel appeared, a few yards away, and started to progress towards her. She stiffened, then the personnel asked her candidly: "Are you Vitoli?" She responded back rather timidly: "Yes, I am." The personnel instructed her to follow them to the police station, stating that they had something to ask her. The police personnel told her to change her school uniforms and take some food if she was hungry. She went to her place, drank a cup of milk, and followed them to the police station, without changing her uniform. When Vitoli saw his brother and his friends, at the police station, she was much relieved.

The police began interrogating the siblings. It wasn't a strange whim – the essence of detaining them concerned the two elder brothers, Kaito and Kughato Sukhai. They were asked to reveal their brothers' hideout, which was followed by torrents of dull probing. All the siblings could reply was that they had not heard from them for a year or so. After a rapid round of questioning, Vikuto and Vitoli were locked up in separate blocks. To worsen the horrid event, Vitoli was locked up with some mentally deranged inmates, and she had a hard time surviving. The food was nauseating, the plates were filthy, and Vitoli thought that even animals would be better fed than that. She wondered why anyone would be treated this way. Almost on the edge of losing her mind, Vitoli pondered, how long she could endure such treatment. She convinced herself to be strong in order to reunite with her family one day.

The very next day, the Naga students in Shillong learned of the arrest of the two siblings, from a local newspaper, and decided to pay them a visit. Among the visitors was a Naga lad named Lanu Longchar, who would later become a well-known preacher in Naga Hills. Lanu was busy taking pictures of the two Naga prisoners with his newly acquired Kodak camera. He was unaware that keen eyes were prying on him. It wasn't long until the personnel seized his camera and started to accuse him: "Why are you taking pictures of these prisoners? Are you a spy sent by General Kaito? Did he send you to take these pictures?"

Without any valid evidence, Lanu Longchar was locked up with the other Naga inmates.

Although curbed and relegated to times of misery, sometimes, getting together with Lanu would spur a beam of smiles upon the faces of the Naga inmates. They would teasingly taunt him: "Hey dear Lanu, did you get our pictures right?" and together they would have a hearty laugh. The following weeks, they heard some news about the transferring of Naga inmates to Kohima prison. They became so elated, despite being in captivity, as the sense of moving closer to their native homes, and treading on their own soil, incited a feeling akin to their having been set free. The rumour turned out to be true and they were soon transferred to Kohima jail.

The grisly torturing at Kohima was no different from Shillong. Beating was a daily business at Kohima. Vikuto was brutally beaten up and was asked to disclose the hideouts of his brother Kaito and Kughato. In fact, Vikuto had no knowledge about his brothers' whereabouts. The last time they had met was a year previous, before he left for Shillong. His lack of knowledge on his brothers went unheeded, he said, "I am just a student, and I have been staying at Shillong for a while. It is you who should know about them."

The police did not deem the lad was telling the truth, and he was beaten to pulp. However, in the end, they accepted that Vikuto was indeed telling the truth. Apart from the endless torture and misery, it was also a moment of solace for the siblings, in Kohima jail, because they could see each other, after quite a long time.

On Left: One of the authors, Khekaho Zhimomi, – after the interview with Vikuto Zhimomi. On Right: the younger brother of General Kaito and the Chairman of the Joint Forum of Nagaland GBs (Chieftains) and Dobashis (Custodian of customary Law) Federation.

The nightmare did not end there as their succour was short-lived. Within weeks, news was circulating that, soon, retransferring to another prison was going to take place. The minute Vitoli heard the news, her nightmare once again resumed. She pleaded with the Kohima prison authorities that they should be transferred to anywhere but Shillong.

Much to Vitoli's relief, it wasn't the Shillong Jail, she had dreaded, it was the Naogoan (formerly Nowgong) special jail at Assam. This prison was consigned, mainly, to political offenders: inmates being those who were charged with sedition, treason and abetting the insurgency, etc.

The temperature inside the jail was unbearable, mosquitoes were plenty, food was unhealthy, and sickness was inevitable. In those days, fans and coolers were unheard of and inmates would simply cool off their sizzling sun-scorched bodies by splashing cold water. Without any certainty of their fate, days, weeks and months passed. Engulfed in pain and misery, anticipation of their release became a daily routine. Vitoli was left in a cesspool of despair.

The presence of several key prisoners in the Nagoan District Jail had the benefit of some VIPs dropping by more often. Visitors ranged from top bureaucrats, to ministers and even Chief Minister on some special holidays. On one such favourable occasion the Governor of Assam, Fazal Ali, accompanied by his daughter, chanced upon to pay a visit to this fateful jail.

Fortunately, the Governor and his daughter met this ill-fated schoolgirl. Vitoli by then had shrunken into a bare skeletal form, with just a thin strip of frayed clothing casing her emaciated body. Vitoli started to narrate her story to the Governor and his daughter. She related how, without justification she and her brothers were being held captives. She also spoke about the plight of her father and her younger brother who was being confined to Jorhat District jail and Kohima jail, respectively, and how her other family members were scattered in different places. God only knew if they were even alive. Her list seemed endless; she further told the Governor that if what she heard was true, then, her father, who was in Jorhat Jail, had been treated poorly, and was succumbing, devoid of proper cell, foods and poor hygiene, etc. If truth be told, Kuhoto was reduced to skin and bones. Vitoli's tears started rolling down as she whispered: "Just because my father took the side of his own people does not mean that he is a criminal. Even if he has to be imprisoned, he deserves a decent treatment."

The Governor's daughter listened to Vitoli's account intently and started to weep. She was immensely moved by the story of this young girl and her family. The Governor was also moved by the trouble experienced by this genial girl. He assured Vitoli that he would look into her father's case. Later, it was learned that the Governor Shri. Fazal Ali had indeed made some calls to Jorhat District jail, and subsequently, until his release, her father was no longer deprived of the privileges due to a political prisoner.

During those gruelling times, which the Kuhoto family endured, Phizo's family also went through similar affliction: Phizo's wife, Jwenle, with her young son Zasozo still on her lap, daughter Adino, and niece Rano M. Shaiza with her infant child, and her husband Lumshing Shaiza, were all confined to Naogoan district jail, at the same. In fact, many suffered and numerous individuals gave up their lives, but the hardship and misery gone through by these two families, during the Naga freedom-struggle journey was, without doubt, the hardest.

"The most heart-rending episode during the time in Naogoan jail," as Vitoli pensively recalls was when her father, who was in Jorhat Jail, sent across a comb made out of bamboo, and a note, through one of the inmates, who had been recently transferred from Jorhat to Naogoan jail. The letter reads:

> My dear daughter Avi [nickname for Vitoli], do not lose your spirit yet, for God shall never abandon us. Today, we are suffering an immense misery, but tomorrow we will relish the fruits of today's agony. It is my belief that our suffering shall not be in vain, because one day our Naga Hills will shine like the brightest stars of all.

It is a sad fate that Kuhoto is not alive to see his cherished vision of an independent Naga, but it is a firm belief that someday his descendants shall taste the fruits of the tree he planted.

After being confined in Naogoan jail, from 1956 to 1957, a miraculous fate transpired. With the involvement of Governor Fazal Ali, a businessman from Naogoan was made to bail out Vikuto and Vitoli from captivity. Finally, they were released, on bail, after almost two years of imprisonment. Ironically, Vikuto was allowed to take his examination, in prison, and passed his 10th Standard. After their release, the sibling could not be sent back to Naga Hills, since they had no home and no one with whom to stay. Therefore, Vitoli was kept in foster care, at Shillong, for three months, at the Governor's personal security officer Captain Sethi's house, where she stayed along with his daughter, Manju. Vitoli's brother Vikuto was admitted into a hostel at Shillong and continued his studies. Kuhoto was released from Jorhat District jail after completing his one-and-a-half-year sentence. He returned to the village, only to find his wife, Kiholi, still lodged at Zhekiye village concentration camp, and his youngest son, Kuhoi, and his daughter, Hotoli, still hiding with their elder brothers, Kaito and Kughato, with the Indian troops were hunting them, incessantly. Kuhoto gradually sank into a severe mental depression. He kept on asking where his youngest son was. And indeed, a few days later, the youngest son, Kuhoi, was called from hiding to meet his father, and evidently seeing his youngest son gladdened Kuhoto to some extent. Thereafter, Kuhoi was send to Shillong to continue his schooling. Kuhoto died in 1972.

A recent picture of Vitoli Hoky, General Kaito's youngest sister, with her husband, Dr. Hokishe Yepthomi.

Six

His Inspiration to nationalism and the era of his fighters

General Kaito's inspiration towards Naga nationalism can be ascribed to a few individuals. Categorically, his number one influence would be none other than his elder brother Kughato Sukhai. This man was an outstanding speaker, and an impeccable and competent statesman. He loved Naga people from the core of his heart, without any prejudices, and was in turn valued and loved even more by his people. He was one of the primary figures among the Naga nationalists, on their venture for self-determination. In effect, Kughato Sukhai set the first record in the history of Naga struggle. As a mark of Naga independence, he hoisted the first Naga National flag at Kohima, on 14 August 1947, one day prior to Indian Independence Day. This was a deed which no one else offered to perform. Kaito, while still a teenager, would attentively take note of his eldest brother's account of Naga struggles, in fact, he was never tired of listening to them. He would gradually imbibe the nationalist ideology and amass an enormous amount of facts on the affairs of the movement, from his brother, while he himself would soon become the main protagonist of this movement.

Late Kughato Sukhai also known as J.K. Sukhai, the eldest brother of General Kaito Sukhai and the Ato Kilonser (Prime Minister) of the Federal Government of Nagaland.

General Kaito was deeply inspired by his great-grandfather Sukhai Zhimomi, the fearless and dreaded warlord in his era, Sukhai's spirited character seemed to have permeated into Kaito and become manifest in his passion and drive.

Another great personality to have preceded and inspired Kaito was his granduncle Kuhoi Sema Naga who led about 2,000 Naga Labour troops to Europe, in 1917 and displayed unrivalled bravery, in World War I. With only his conventional weapons, machete and spear, he participated in the warfare and despite the sophisticated weaponry, he took 24 heads. It was also recorded that 'Kuhoi was present at 130 enemy deaths in battle.' Kuhoi Sema Naga died in the course of this war, on December 25, 1917, and was buried in Marseilles, France.

Lastly, yet importantly, the praiseworthy contribution of his parents is deemed fit to be placed in the annals of the Naga self-determination movement. Their role was the fuel which kept the flames of the brothers', Kaito's and Kughato's struggles ignited. Kaito's parents,

Kuhoto and Kiholi offered an unwavering moral and material support to their sons and shouldered numerous miseries while treading this harrowing path.

Kaito and his brother Kughato even took on "Sukhai" as their surname in place of Zhimomi. The usage of "Sukhai" as their surname was not down to their ancestor prominence alone, but there was also another obvious reason. The brothers being the central force navigating the massive tide of the Naga National Movement which again was propelled by assorted tribes and clans, and the pair belonging to the Zhimomi clan, their observation was, Zhimomi had been the largest group among the Sümis, in the freedom-struggle initiation era, and lest the sentiment of dominancy over one another sprout again, akin to the earlier head hunting and clannish era, when supremacy was reckoned by the number of people slain or the number of scalps collected, the pair thought that the usage of the surname Zhimomi would definitely overwhelm their purpose and their aspiration, and could bring crashing down the Nation they dreamed to raise. Nagas being a diverse clump of tribes, they also mulled over the possibility that, the slanderers would perhaps use it as the ingredient to incite distrust and enmity among the brotherhood. This did actually transpire, at one point in time.

At the pinnacle of their headship, the time when Kughato was the Ato Kilonser (Prime Minister) of FGN and Kaito was the Commander-in-chief of the Federal Naga Army, some opposing elements made-up a report that the Zhimomi brothers were planning to create their own Government. The gossip, was later exposed as farce, a ploy purely intended to topple the leadership. As a matter of fact, it did create disarray amid the brotherhood to some extent. But they subdued the sense of prevailing supremacy practiced between the clans in the time of yore, so as to instil the oneness among the Sümis in particular and Nagas in general to jointly fight against the real enemy beyond their realm. The glory days of his ancestor defending the clans from adversaries had long gone but the stories were still fresh in Kaito's mind. Once again, in his new era, the destiny has ushered in a far greater liability for him to shoulder. This time he wouldn't just be fighting for his clansmen or his tribesmen, he would be fighting against the foreign regime for the entire 60 or so segregated tribes of the Nagas.

***

A journey of thousand miles begins with a single step, and along this great journey of freedom struggle, the Naga fighters diligently marched ahead. While they still had miles to go, arriving at that point was akin to how droplets of will could breed belief into a vast span of hope. The gallant feats displayed at the preceding battles, by the young leader, and the merging of the Naga Safe Guards and the Home Guards into the Naga National Army, after the declaration of the Federal Government of Nagaland, had encouraged the youths to join this movement with even greater zeal. Trumpets were blown, now that they were stirred and transfused with the notion that overthrow of foreign rule over the ancestral land was a possibility. It was their burden to strike the blow and fend the Movement with all they had. Gradually, Kaito had been carefully preparing a powerful armed rebellion group called the 'Naga Safe Guards', which on 22 March 1956, united with Naga Home Guards to serve as military wing of Federal Government of Nagaland. In the initial stages, the Naga Safe Guards was barely a militia made up of a few dedicated partners of Kaito, but gradually, it grew into a widespread formation, which became a fully-fledged National Army, always growing and becoming more powerful. Creating this army was never easy. It was raised on the pedestal of blood, sweat, tears, passion, courage and loyalty. It was honed out of blunt warriors who transformed into refined deadly trained fighters. This creation was indeed a perfect illustration of the leap of faith.

In April 1956, the make-shift headquarter of Naga fighters at Xuivi village had to be vacated, and was shifted to an imposing hill, at the old Shena village, Zunheboto, some 20 miles away from Xuivi, because the Indian troops were riled by the humiliating raid inflicted on their police post at old Satakha village by Kaito and his men. The Satakha episode left the Indian troops completely abashed and revenge was inevitable. The new Naga Army Garrison at old Shena was brimming with life. Gates were open 24-7, and youths flooded the gateway, waiting in queues, eager to draft into the newly formed national army. The camp was crammed with activities and the new recruits were toiling frantically.

Hitherto, Kaito and his *avant-gardes* militia were no more than twelve soldiers, but the flame he roused couldn't be doused, as of now the trickle had incited a huge wave or rather a full-scale war between the Nagas and the Indian troops. Naga fighters, consisting mostly of youths, were prepared to sacrifice their education, no matter what befell their families or themselves in order to defend their Nation from foreign domination. At times, the families of Naga-army members were tortured, physically and mentally, to reveal their whereabouts.

Bearing in mind these certain threats, a number of senior leaders at the launch of the Naga army were quite nervous about Kaito's move. They were very aware of the reality that Nagas would be an unequal opponent to a mammoth nation like India, if physical attacks were to be taken into account. Nevertheless, Kaito had gone with a bang. He lit the flame overnight and displayed the fireworks – the just essence of what people could become when their freedom was under threat. In response to Kaito's move, and spirited as they were, quick as a bolt, Nagas awakened to the stark reality. They were prepared to do just about anything, to overthrow the Indian troops' oppression. The most surprising outcome was the teamwork within the Nagas, who until then had been fighting an inter-tribal fight, but now had the hope of fighting cohesively against the common enemy, which of course was a great momentum, which meant that they had already won the first battle.

In many places, Kaito's men rampantly attacked the police post established by the Assam state. At Satakha police post, they captured all the bewildered policemen, stripped them of clothes, and ordered them to parade back to their place. At that moment, the enemy was left in pessimistic mode, and this is what Nagas had sought. In the milieu of huge arms haul at Satakha and the account of riveting feats at the battle of Hoshepu, the movement was gathering momentum amidst the wider Naga community. And, however tiny the Indians considered them to be, Nagas, for the time being were resting on a green couch with sparkling glee, for they were on the offensive and at par with formidable foes. The enemy was feeling tense and troubled. The Indian troops had deluged almost every Naga village and the fighters' dwelling abodes. They were brutal because they were on a mission with orders right from on high. But after a while, the fighters were braced and on a rigid footing to absorb the assault.

On learning of the unrestrained surge in attacks that ensued, without further ado, in September 1956, the Indian government sent General K.S. Thimaya to the Naga Hills, to initiate talks and pacify the heated Naga fighters. By 18 September, General Thimaya arrived at Ghukiye village, Zunheboto. This particular area was a nucleus where the pulsating forces were being raised and the conciliation therefore had to be scheduled here. General Thimaya had a meeting with Kughato Sukhai, who was then the Angh of Sümi region. Nihoi Jakhalu, the personal assistant to the Deputy Commissioner of Zunheboto, accompanied Gen. Thimaya to Ghukiye village and interpreted the talk between the two leaders. They agreed to have a truce for one week.

At the meeting, General Thimaya's opening question to Kughato was "What do you think of the future of the Nagas?"

Without hesitation, Kughato answered, "The future of the Nagas is bright, if only the government of India leaves them alone."

General Thimaya next told Kughato, "The Government of India has sent me here to understand your desire."

Kughato said, "If that is so, then, tell your Government to recognize our sovereignty", to which General Thimaya responded, "I will convey to my government whatever you ask me, though, I cannot assure you about the sovereignty."

Kughato, then said, "The present freedom movement is not an individual issue. The desire of the Nagas is to restore their sovereignty. Will not your Government admit the truth?"

Then, General Thimaya jigged the conversation into somewhat brag of a sort, "I will give you fifteen days. Can you talk to other Nagas?"

The banter steadily turned into seeming aggravation between the two leaders.

Kughato snapped back, "Do you think Nagas will surrender their sovereignty just within fifteen days?"

Gen. Thimaya evaded the question and said, "What do you think personally?"

Kughato retorted, "Even if the Indian authorities use all their forces and arrest me or kill me, they cannot arrest or kill the right of the Nagas."

Thimaya concluded saying rather pompously, "Since it's a rule, when your soldiers and my soldiers attack each other or happen to capture or kill any one of us, we should not feel guilt for that."

Kughato replied firmly, "Not at all. There is no other choice."

That was the end of a significant encounter between the two leaders.

One fascinating thing that occurred in the course of this meeting was Gen. Thimaya said, "Mr. Sukhai", and placed half a rupee coin on the table, suavely suggesting something lesser than full independence. Kughato's presence of mind being pretty amazing, he reacted right away, to the gesture of the Indian general, by taking out a full rupee coin from his pocket and placing it on top of Gen. Thimaya's half-rupee coin, implying that Nagas would resolve for no less than full independence. They understood each other's mind. The meeting served no purpose and the two leaders dispersed in rather dismal mood.

After failing to agree terms, the armistice, which had been agreed for one week, between the Naga army and Indian forces, was reduced to a day. Next day, on September 20, more intensified fighting between the two belligerent groups resumed. The Naga Army bastion, at old Shena village, was heavily bombarded, with mortars being fired by the Indian forces stationed at Ghukiye village. However, shortly after the meeting fiasco, and before the shelling began, with great insight, the Naga fighters had shifted their camps to a safer zone, while the villagers as well, had fled from the area, which was why there were no casualties.

General Kaito was utterly annoyed by the volume of military menace brought into the Naga Hills by General Thimaya. He ridiculed and belittled the cannons of Indian troops; "Never bother about being shelled by random firing with large calibre cannons. Cannons will thunder but they'll hardly kill Nagas. Cannons will roar but will swallow nobody."

Furthermore, he boosted the morale of his soldiers saying, "Comrades, truly, I assure you, our sparingly used rifles will be more effective in hitting targets than the random firing of Indian-army cannons."

Kaito was mindful that Indian troops would in fact march to the bombarded fortress, soon after they have poured heavy artillery from a safe distance. Therefore, he rallied his troops and motivated them quite snootily, "Come, my able fighters, our chance to display that one hundred Indians are no match for three Naga soldiers has arrived. I have personally surveyed a three-kilometre radius of our stronghold, and also marked ten strategic positions where you could place yourselves and lay an ambush to recover enemy guns."

Indeed, in this event, General Kaito was preparing to display the prowess of the underrated tribal martial skills to General Thimaya and his troops. He had deployed his fighters at every striking end to cripple down the enemy forces and capture a stash of arms and ammunition. It was a sheer luck that the Indian troops were warned by their intelligence agents before the young general's plan could be executed. They heeded the cautions. If they had not, marching to the Naga bastion would have entwined them in General Kaito's bloodbath web. The young general was very disappointed. A more upsetting incident would occur, the following week, in the adjoining Lotha Naga region. On 6 November, 1956, one of the bravest of General Kaito's commanders, Lieutenant General Yambemo Patton, who was popularly nicknamed 'Yambemo' (the lion heart) among his fellow soldiers, was killed at N. Longidang village, Wokha, by the Indian troops, after a fierce gun battle, between them and the Naga fighters.

At the beginning of the struggle, the Indian government termed the Naga nationalists as 'dacoits', thugs and terrorists. However, following the epic battle of Hoshepu, and the siege at Satakha, they were labelled 'hostiles'. They were not described as freedom fighters until the failed conciliation, or rather the rational confrontation between General Thimaya and Kughato at Ghukiye. Right after this event, the insightful General Thimaya submitted to Prime Minister Jawaharlal

Lal Nehru in his reports that: Nagas have a political problem and not a military problem. Gradually, Naga fighters were recognised as Nationalists.

Despite repeated successful exploits, one thing of which Nagas were certain was, that they would be drained of energy sooner or later, as would be their limited war supplies. Hence, to sustain the movement, they sought a complementary way as well. In a little while, NNC-FGN held a number of secret discussions. The most important meeting took place at Sanis, in Lotha Naga country. The get-together at Sanis was solely to consider the issues which pertained to the dire needs for external aid, to support the Naga freedom struggle. Speaking of other ways and meant it was time to tell the world about Naga sufferings; time to send out a flare, since they had awoken the giant and it seemed the latter would settle for nothing less than a strong assault. India could not be taunted. It had become apparent that Naga influences alone could not override the Indians. Yet, the big query was who would bell the cat and achieve the impossible. Someone among the revolutionaries would have to move out for the political kill, a person be skilled enough for the job. Several members of the Movement were willing to go out, but most people thought Phizo would be the most credible. Phizo was the most senior amongst the nationalists and without doubt an astute leader.

The NNC President was chosen to be sent out but there were scores of problems. Firstly, how could anyone navigate through the thick chain of Indian security walls without being noticed? Indian troops were everywhere. Nagas could hide indefinitely, in the home terrain, but going out, in unfamiliar places, was full of risks. If the Naga fighters Intelligence could squeeze the Indians and their spies, the Indian Intelligence could do the same. Secondly, even if they could possibly slip out through the border, the hope of obtaining neighbouring friends was still vague, for they had never previously ventured out.

However, having considered the odds, Phizo consented to attempt the mission. A number of meetings were held, and an escape route was skilfully worked out, to enable Phizo navigate out of the Indian Territory, to Bangladesh, erstwhile East Pakistan. In the opinion of the Nagas, East Pakistan was the closest neighbour, a rival of India, and unlikely to refuse them assistance.

Phizo, along with Khodao Yanthan and Yonkong Nganshi, were escorted to East Pakistan by a band consisting of 25 bodyguards led by two senior officers Lt Col. Tsemomo Lotha and Captain Toshisho Naga. Toshiho was then serving as General Kaito's personal security officer. In the escort team were also two other competent Naga rebel Intel officers, Inspector Tadingpou Gangmei and Intelligence Director, Zhekuto Sema. Prior to Phizo's departure from India, cash was collected for his expenses. Under the direction of FGN, a substantial sum was collected from the Sümi villages and their neighbourhood. Zuheto Swu, who was GOC of Eastern command, was entrusted with this job. Kaito's youngest brother Kuhoi, then very young but full of zest, vividly remembers following Zuheto on this job. The duo individually collected a huge sum of money for Phizo's expenditure; the money was submitted to Phizo at Phonkhuri Naga village in the Burmese border and despite the dual fold security operation initiated to hem in Phizo by both the Indian regular troops and Naga village guard groomed by the Indian authorities, the NNC leader slipped out deftly, and safely landed at East Pakistan.

The pendulum was rocked, and the onus rested on Phizo to obtain new friends in the external circle, while leaders like Kughato, Scato and Kaito were given the massive task of running the de-facto government on the domestic front to flout the iron fist of the Indian union. Kaito, then a promising young leader was pretty self-assured towards his mission; he was well aware that the Indian authority shall not rest content unless they snuff out the newly formed Naga Federal Government. The solemn pledge Kaito took to protect his government and his people from the Indian aggression was a vow not to be taken lightly. Therefore, in the face of every threat or pain, there is no way he was going to let his people down. The harsh terrain which has a strange savour to most outside aggressors would serve as his primary weapon against his giant foe. Some Indian forces would later agree to the fact that fighting with Nagas on their rugged and irregular thick jungles was indeed a second Vietnam. The Vietnamese rebels used their intractable grounds to their great advantage on their almost two decades 'war of tragedy' against the United States.

The departure of the British from Hills, and the dawn of Indians had opened up new hostility. Although Nagas were not geared up quite as much in modern weapons or physical numbers in contrast to their mighty enemy, they were, nevertheless, not deprived of the greatest human weapon that has ever been wielded, which is 'the courage of the heart.' Nagas were strong-willed and ever prepared. For centuries they had been fighting off and on, which was why the fighter instincts were natural in them. Following the formation of the Naga army, Gen. Kaito Sukhai and his followers started beating a war drum. He clicked a violent stroke with double speed and went berserk, striking shocks wherever he went with his soldiers. His first move was seizing the enemy's weapons and then using the captured guns and ammunition against them. A number of elders were worried about this man; they said, "This man had about him an air of natural charisma," rumour has it that some magnetism was affixed to this young leader." At his instant call, many people old and young, would willingly yield to his influence and join his fighting group. His devotees say they would follow wherever he led them. When Kaito shouts, "Where are my Atsulis?" he meant 'action.' "Atsuli" means 'watchdog.' Zukiye Zhimomi, Vitomo Lithsami, Jehoto Kulhopu and Vikuho Zhimomi were four of his well-known watchdogs. Among them was Zukiye, the most decorated fighter among the ranks of Kaito's brave officers; it is believed that he was the only Naga officer who was exempt from saluting any of his superiors if he didn't wish to.

Lt. Colonel Zukiye Zhimomi, the most decorated commander among the ranks of General Kaito's officers, he was also called the Atsuli (the Watchdog) of General Kaito.

Almost immediately, Naga Hills was plagued with freedom fighters. Indian Intelligence watchdogs were mystified; they couldn't keep up with the briskness of systematic plunder, arsons, threats and assaults meted to the Assam police. Life was difficult for these police forces; they were either running helter-skelter or either locked up inside their besieged camps. It was indeed the glorious phase for the Naga fighters. Apparently, some prospect was in the offing. The Indian union was now left between a rock and a hard place. They had to either contain these fighters or yield to their demands. But containing them seemed rather a far cry. An adrenaline rush was already driving this young leader. What the Indian troops couldn't understand was, the more they pushed in, the more Naga fighters were becoming aggressive and stronger with greater numbers. It seemed that for every one they took out, more appeared. Gen. Kaito instructed his men, "If you go to the villages, do not stay undercover, let them know that we are all over the place." The motive was to shock their rivals, wherever they went. Tiredness Kaito had none. He could do without sleep and rest for several days, yet he never took a stimulant or a cup of tea, but amazingly, weariness never showed in his eyes. He led a frugal life energised with the heart of a warrior ship; "Never beat a retreat, even if you have to sacrifice yourself," was how he often inspired his trusted followers. He would say, "For my motherland, I could fight to the death."

After the formation of the Federal Government, the Naga Hills was literally swarming with Kaito's followers, stirring the masses to join the movement so as to create more chaos and disorder for the Indian government. They were scattered at almost every place, in particular, trailing the armed police forces, waiting for an opportune instant to snatch away their guns and bullets. In no time, there appeared to be a large number of weapons in the arsenals of the Naga fighters. The Indian government sentries combing the area, went about with their guns chained to their bodies for the rebels frequently emerged out of nowhere and snatched away their weapons at the drop of a hat. Pro-government officials who ventured out on their administrative duties were the most vulnerable ones. During the daytime they would be followed and guarded by jeeps loaded with Assam police or village guards; at dusk, they were clogged up inside their government bungalow, probably yearning to see the dawn.

Kaito's versatile fighters were taking Assam police in their stride. And with the Nagas starting to overpower them, Delhi was somewhat startled and blew a gasket. Perhaps, these tribal fighters mustn't be taken for granted. Almost immediately, the Assam police was removed from the scene, and in place the Indian Regular Operational Forces took the reins. By April 1956, they moved into the Naga Hills. Without much of a clue, half a year was estimated by the Indian forces to flush out the Naga insurgency. By and large this is what was predicted considering the numbers and fire-power. However, the dilemma remained; first, they were penetrating unfamiliar territory. It was an extreme convoluted zone inhabited by a mishmash of tribal people, so they had to use discretion. India could not be an exploitive nation in the eyes of the world as she had only recently been freed from the yoke of British exploitation after her tedious Non-violence campaign against them. The government order was to shoot only when shot at. The conflict of interest was, would it be possible to pursue the order given by the higher-ups? It was not likely. At times there prevailed a tricky-situation for the Indian forces. There was no pattern or variation between the regular villagers and the real fighters; all seemed to be identical. They couldn't tell which ones were fighters and which were not. In addition, if the first sequence of orders were to be followed, they had to be careful; the ordinary villager mustn't be angered. Further, they were utterly frustrated by the subtle nature of the Naga fighters; time and again they slipped through their dragnets. The matter was getting trickier with each passing day.

The battle on the Hills was ensuing gravely, with the Nagas frequently on the offensive. In the meantime, the Indian Parliament session was once again rocked with fury. A frenzied debate took place and the majority voted in favour of a bill known as the Armed Forces Special Powers Act (AFSPA). The act is still in effect to the present day. Naga Hills was declared as a disturbed area by September 11, 1958, and the Armed Forces Special Powers Act was enforced in the Naga Hills. The Indian forces were pretty wary of their zigzag area of operation, but leaving aside this setback and given the more unbridled power in the form of AFSPA, they were still confident. Before they even moved in, they proudly demeaned the Naga fighters to nothing more than a sheer bunch of gangsters and outlaws, presuming that containing crude jungle trained Naga fighters would take no time at all. On the other hand, Kaito used this undervalued assumption to his advantage. While they assumed he was naïve, he was actually preparing for any eventuality that they had in store for him. He doled out his sparse forces into five major commands - eastern, western, southern, northern and the central command; it consisted of 3 divisions and 28 battalions. To be specific, Kaito scattered his men everywhere.

The birth of the AFSPA, endowed a great deal of power into the Indian military's hands, especially in the Northeast region. It also augmented the total number of forces deployed. In simple terms, the Act can be labelled as the iron claw and fang with built-in retribution to any transgressions committed. Naga Hills then became the world's most dense area of military operation. A new strategy was charted to draw the line between the fighters and common people. Even prior to the AFSPA, the might of the Indian Army was felt in many parts of the Hills, more so in the Sümi Naga country, which was flooded with armed forces. Now, they extended over the entire Hills. The Indian troops were reinforced and more alert. The first plan was to differentiate between the common people and fighters; but how? The answer is not as easy as it sounds; they had to restrict the ordinary villagers so as to cut-off the essential supplies to the fighters, which until then, were being provided by the ordinary people. The next step is to hunt down the fighters. They were going to play hard at the risk of killing the innocent.

Sooner than expected, they started clamping down firmly on the ordinary villagers. They were concentrated in groups; movements were heavily restricted, granaries were burnt down and fields were left unattended, which rendered the villagers severely depleted and hungry. Whatever little was left on their holding, was burnt to the ground. Most went fleeing into the thick jungles, hiding with their entire families for fear of Indian torture and incarceration. While in hiding, there have been numerous stories of the villagers feeding and surviving on assorted wild fruits, yam, roots, etc.... Countless people, mostly children, died during the operation due to starvation or epidemics. While in concentration camps, which to this day was also referred to by the locals as groupings, the detainees were humiliated, severely tortured and killed. One of the few such incidents to share is, Pastor Pelesato Chase, the caretaker of the Phezu Mission Centre at Bible Hill, was tortured day and night and afterwards put inside a sack and burned to death by the callous 14th Assam Rifles Regiment. The immoral appetite of these soldiers was outrageous; women were raped pitilessly; even the elderly, the minors, the unwell and the crippled were unsafe. Every family was left scarred; hearts were broken, yet there was no end to these unspeakable tragedies. Imagine an infant being snatched away from its mother's arms only to be smashed to death! The afflictions went beyond human tolerance. But despite of all the pains and sufferings, many determined fighters did not waver in their resolve or cower to the enemy's threats. Some lingered in the jungle to a period of two to three years.

Other than a few government officials, the Naga Hills of 1956 to 1964 was the last place on earth people wanted to be; it was like Hitler's Germany. The torment inflicted upon the Nagas during that period, was in fact the most painful episode in the historical testimony of the Naga people, and perhaps the biggest human rights blunder committed thus far by the Indian forces. The reckless nightmare was concealed in the eyes of the outer world; India has caused suffering and taken delight in it. But with the passing of time and after dozens of fruitless negotiations or rather disinclined accords, an incident known as the 1987 'Oinam Massacre' came onto the radar of some human rights activists. They termed the Indian action as unruly and tyrannical. The activists interrupted meetings and hurled abusive accusations at the Indian government. The voice of Naga's distress proclaimed to the outside nations by the Naga Federal leaders in the earlier part of the events fell on deaf ears. On the other hand, even with the intervention of various external bodies, India did not acknowledge or show any remorse for their action. Rather, they were inclined towards conceit and deceit. "Naga's war was no bigger than a familial issue and hence should be settled within the ambit of Indian union," which to the Nagas, was a blatant lie.

With the restricted movement of the villagers, the fighters were severed from their essential needs. Naga fighters were now turning to defensive mode; they could hide for an indefinite period, but not without food. This gave some breathing space to the Indian forces for the time being. Accordingly, the Indian counter insurgency operation started moving ahead towards a definite plan in the Indian administered Naga territory. But either way, Kaito was undeterred; he was steps ahead of the enemy. He had made ready another means. A nestling hideout for his fighters was already being prepared across

Myanmar's border; all the enemy could do was watch with contempt, as they had limited access beyond the border. The Naga fighters could easily travel into Manipur Naga country, and then spread out into Burmese Naga terrain.

Despite many twists, the race is to the swift. Indian forces never ceased to ease their pace, as Kaito's fighters would certainly use their least relaxation to their benefit, and there's no way the Indian Army would welcome that. To Kaito's reckoning, the landscape kept consuming the Indian troops. Each hill had its eyes, and every jungle had its ears. During the day, the presence of Indian soldiers would be spotted either by Naga women working in the fields or the children playing in the fringes. They, in turn, beckoned the active one among them to run subtly and notify the Naga fighters nestling nearby. Once the information reached the fighters, they would either sneak away to their hideout or lay an ambush on the position where the enemies were heading, which depended on the number of enemy troops in the area. If the number was more than they could handle, they would simply disappear into their burrows; if it was lesser, then vice versa. Even in the present day, no outsider could cross the threshold of a Naga village without the knowledge of its people. Nagas have been safeguarding their land and skirmishing in intertribal feuds from time immemorial; therefore, consistent alertness was natural to them.

The nights were very dangerous for the Indian troops. By day, Naga fighters would shrink back to their burrows. After dusk, like nocturnal creatures, they crawled out noiselessly, and all activities would be set in motion. Driven by responsibility and otherwise beset with doleful spirits, the Indian troops patrolled on duty with fear. It seemed they were fighting an unseen enemy. In most encounters they would find themselves outmanoeuvred by Naga troops and a myriad of them were taken out in the dark. Unreported by the newspapers and reporters, the Indian defence ministry fatality register was rapidly filling up. While the dead bodies of anonymous soldiers still sleep peacefully on an unmarked grave somewhere in the fringes of the Naga villages, how was it even possible? Until then, the Indian forces were chipping away these at these mountain warriors whom they regarded as nothing more than a bunch of outlaws. Now they were utterly bowled; they were amazed by the acumen and audacity harnessed by this young leader and his faithful followers. Kaito was just out of his teens, and the respect he commanded among the ranks was truly astonishing. It was the phase when Naga fighters were regularly on the winning side, and Gen. Kaito was armed to the teeth.

In days past, Nagas used the technique of lighting bonfires to alert or send messages to the far-flung villages. General Kaito also used this ancient craft against the Indian troops. His men had started a method of a 'lighting alert system.' First, the enemy's presence was instantly relayed to the adjoining ranges by fire beacon signs; then, the signal would monitor the enemy track. Strings of villages and the Naga army hideaway in between the ranges would be alerted, and, depending on the frequency of the signal, the fighters could discern which course they were coming or leaving. They would then either lay an attack or swiftly vanish from the area. There were also other methods like the 'visual clue system' used by the Naga fighters. It indicated the direction, the numbers and the timing of the Indian forces patrolling in the area. As strange as it may seem, Kaito brought the ancient and modern method of combat together and used it skilfully against his superior rival. To the amazement of Indian forces, they could only unravel his crafty ways of warfare in the latter part of the encounters. Many would later describe Kaito as one of the greatest military strategists of his time.

The Indian government had more than enough troops to contain the fighters. However, given the nature of the harsh terrain, it bothered them to deploy their forces in regular form and therefore they had to operate in small streaks. With the casualty rate rising during that period, the common observation was that if any of the Indian soldiers were to stay for an extended period in the Naga Hills, the chances of his survival would be slim. The Indian army mainly consisted of younger soldiers on their first assignment. Trails were perilous; sharp bamboo traps were strewn everywhere, the jungle had ears, their presence was felt the instant they stepped into motion, so surprise attacks were always certain. Fear stalked them wherever they tread; the sight and smell of death would frequently engulf them; the first and the last in line rarely returned from patrol. Terrains were certainly taking a toll on the enemy. The Naga Hills then was considered to be India's Pandora's box. The closer they edged in towards the revolutionaries or the further they sought to buy off some pro-mutineers with an attempt for forced union, then somewhere, as its payback, more surprising troubles would start to emanate. It was indeed strange times, the hunters were being hunted, and the era of Naga fighters had gloriously begun.

In the midst of this action, Kaito's name was rumbling over the Hills and beyond. Among the natives, he had become a household name. He had turned into a legend all at once. Parents in the Sümi region had even begun to christen their children after Kaito. Top brass Indian leaders, at the very mention of his name, would clench their fists and seethe with rage. The name never ceased to ring a bell for the rivals. It wasn't a secret any longer; it was now a disclosed secret. It was reported that any soldiers who got Kaito, dead or alive, could earn the highest Indian gallantry award – a gamble a soldier would risk his life for. Kaito's fame far surpassed the other Naga national fighters. A mischievous devil of a man, Kaito, in one incident, under disguise, even played a football match for the local team against the Indian Brigade Team at his native hometown, Zunheboto. Only after the friendly match finished, and Kaito amusingly moved out to his den did the Indian troops come to learn of the young leader guts. They dreaded and reviled him, but seemingly admired him too. Who was this guy? What was in him? The questions run long. Their curiosity was logical!

They exchanged bullets and accusations but in reality, Indian soldiers knew well that Nagas have every reason to fight back. While they would have done the same if the latter were in their shoes. They were at constant daggers drawn, but there was also some point of time where the Indian troops started considering Nagas as their worthy opponent. Somewhere deep inside the Indian soldiers' hearts existed genuine admiration for Naga fighters.

There's an exception to some rules, and hence it wasn't strange that in some cases, a sense of obligation clearly existed between the two warring groups. One such incident was: a Naga commander somewhere in the Sümi Naga area had developed an eye infection which was getting worse with the passing days. The head men of a particular village informed the Indian army camp officer that the Naga commander wants to meet him. The head men told the officer, "I will lead you to the rendezvous point." The next day, the Indian commander got into his jeep without carrying weapons, and along with the village head man, they headed for the meeting. The location was a small pond close to the village. Apparently, the officer had sent out his patrol in advance in case something should happen. Just then, after reaching the meeting point, the Sümi commander swiftly appeared from the jungle with four armed guerrillas. When he got a glimpse of an Indian officer arriving without any weapons, he gestured his men to drop off their guns to the ground. Afterwards, the Naga officer was treated by an Indian army doctor for some days in the Indian army camp. The Indian commander could have captured the guerrilla commander; similarly, the guerrilla commander too had the chance of deceiving the former and may have shot him at first sight. But neither of them did so because, after all, they both believed that trust could well triumph over hatred, and that humanity has priority over everything else. Such are the few glints of humanity on the dark pages of the Naga freedom struggle journey. The incident was never recorded in the

Indian military archives, but it was true. This Indian commander was never ambushed and his area enjoyed much more peace than any other.

Secret agents were deployed everywhere; they watched each other's back. They took stock of developments taking place between the Indian army and the villagers. Detailed information was conveyed to the Naga fighters every now and then. The fighters would respond depending on the nature of the reports received; the aggressive ones would be repaid by strong assaults, while the friendly ones with peace. Desertion among the fighters was not to be taken lightly; it was regarded as being punishable by death. In cases of a traitor taking the side of the enemy, or an Indian-spy caught amidst the guerrillas, which was seldom, but if it did happen, the traitor did not have the comfort of quick death. He would either be starved to death inside a dirt-hole or beaten to death. Such was the unwritten law of the jungle.

If the villager gave a clean sheet to certain Indian officers and his section of soldiers, it was valued much by the Naga fighters operating in the area. In one event, an ambush was carefully laid in the Sümi Naga area. The fighters were tipped off with the news that an army supply convoy would be passing through the area. The plan was flawless; it was just a matter of time before they would attack the convoy. Just as they were expecting, a cavalcade of military jeeps heading for the base camp, started appearing on the scene at the edge of the hill. But conversely, at the last second, the Naga commander raised his hand and gave a screeching halt to an imminent battering. The convoy roared past an apparent casualty. Later the fighters learnt that this was not the actual convoy they'd been expecting. Luckily for them, at the ultimate instant of shelling, the Naga commander spotted the mechanical number of the escort jeep. It belonged to the Indian commander who had earlier treated the Naga commander. The officer had done them no harm; he had treated the villagers with respect, and the Nagas would never return kindness with cruelty. Many such humane incidents went unrecorded in the annals of both warring groups, but they did happen at times. A smooth sea never made a skilled mariner; the Indians too had learned the hard way. Slowly, with the course of rough times and many action-packed encounters, the Indian soldiers learnt the basic ethics of the Naga fighters. And a good number of them eventually adapted to the laws of the jungle.

Even in the face of ordeal or destitution, Kaito's pursuit to drive away the Indians from the Hills was focused. With no sign of waning, Kaito boosted his fighters against the greater odds. He was a fireball; he created mayhem with whatever sparse weapons were left at his stock and carefully used them against the enemy. In August 1960, Gen. Kaito from Chiku, Sati, Naga Federal Headquarter, relayed to his sub-ordinate, Lt. Gen. Zuheto Swu, to meet him soon to talk about an important matter. Swu, was another audacious Sümi commander who was then serving as the GOC of the Eastern command. Kaito told Zuheto that lately, the 14th Assam Rifles Company Headquarters at Thuda had been posing a huge threat for his soldiers operating between the Myanmar and Indian administered Naga territory. It so happened that the Thuda camp personnel were also giving a hard time to the local community nearby. Kaito was always of the opinion that the antidote for such exploitation should be nothing less than strong assault. Calling Zuheto, he told him that, in whatsoever way, they had to attack the Thuda Camp to teach the rival forces a lesson, as well as expel them from the region.

The location of the Indian base camp at Thuda, to be precise, was located at Matikhru, a small Pochury Naga village, Meluri sub-division, under Phek district, Nagaland. It was a tiny village consisting of just around 15 households. The village is flanked on the north by Ukhrul, Manipur, and bordering with Myanmar in the east. It is about 172 km east of the state capital Kohima. Gen. Kaito's base camp at Sati was a well-oiled machine; it thrived with scores of vital activities. The Indian army post established there, mainly countered the Federal Headquarters located at Chikung, and the Naga Army Camp at Sati. Besides, the establishment of Thuda HQ served the extra purpose of restricting the Naga fighters, operating between the eastern flank and the Indian Naga territory.

Following the meeting between the two senior leaders, a frenzied but deliberate plan was formulated for the strike. Around five hundred Naga Fighters were primed for this mission; Gen. Kaito assigned Lt. Gen. Zuheto Swu to organise the attack, while Lt. Col. Kivihe and Lt Col Zukiye were ordered to assist Swu on this vital mission. The Naga fighters were dispersed into four groups - the first under Commander Adjt Capt. Zhevishe Aye, C-in-C staff; the second under Maj. Honizhe, 6th Battalion; third was commanded by Maj. Khughoto, Div. staff and the fourth was led by Capt. Khuoto 1st Battalion. Although the preparation had started earlier on August 14, the actual attack ensued on August 25, 1960, at 4 PM. The Monsoon season was at its peak, and the downpour was heavy, hence the river was flooded to an extent. Before the strike began, Naga fighters had severed off the entire five bridges leading to the Thuda camp region. The motive was to block any reinforcements from other areas. The lack of weapons at the hands of Naga fighters compelled them to take extra precautions and ensure their preparation was faultless. At the onset of the attack, they flung inflammable bombs made from kerosene and petrol into the thatched barracks of the Indian troops, razing most of it. After exchanging blows for a day and night, they ultimately succeeded in surrounding the Thuda Camp.

Nagas enclosed the camp for a number of weeks. They cut off the water supply and food and ammunition inside the camp were exhausted. The movements inside were also restrained, leaving the Indian soldiers in a completely immobile state. This was, however, not the end of the battle. To expect the arrival of reinforcements for the

Indian troops, was a very slim chance, but for some reason they did not give in. Then, the Indian Air force started sending Dakota planes to drop rations, arms, ammunitions, etc. inside the besieged camp. But little did they know, that Nagas would use this as an opportunity to seize a sizable quantity of dropped weapons and rations.

Three Indian army personnel, a Lance Naik, a wireless operator, and one soldier, were killed during the fight. On 26th August 1960, three Dakotas hovered around to drop arms, ammunition and other goods. To those unsophisticated jungle warriors, the sight and sound of the blaring Dakota hovering above, was pretty thrilling and chilling, too, for it wasn't every day that they encountered such flying machines. Each time the plane emerged to drop the goods, it would descend to a certain height, and of course the mystified guerrillas below would mull over the chance that they could touch the edge of the hovering planes with outstretched hands. The orders were clear, "Do not shoot, lest we should give away our positions." However, the lure of planes hovering just above their head seemed too hard to resist. The phenomenon gave a chance to Capt. Zhevishe Aye, and hordes of his other comrades snuggled up inside the trenches to flout orders, and take the chance of shooting at the enemy planes. Most of them were equipped with antique muzzle guns, some with crossbows and arrows, while the remainder with renovated Mark rifles. But it didn't daunt them. In unison, they start to shoot at the airborne beasts and as a result, all three planes were hit by the raining bullets. One flew far towards Burma and then vanished into the deep forest, possibly crashed. The second plane, according to later reports, somehow reached Jorhat, but was badly damaged. The third Dakota with the engine number H.J. 233(G), caught a number of bullets on the engine, spurted slowly around Akhewgo village with thick smoke trailing behind, and then spiralled downward to Tuzu River. The damaged plane plummeted unsteadily and crash landed in the terrace field close to the river bank in the Kulfu village area. Captain Zuheshe Sema was patrolling with his unit in that area when he saw a plane trailed by smoke with blaring sounds plunging into a field. He rushed to the spot with his units and captured the entire nine badly-shaken crew. A pilot named Captain Anand Singhya, (the one who was later described as 'the best Indian pilot of his time,') a Lieutenant, two operators and five droppers were caught without any serious injuries. Content with the spoils, Zuheshe and his comrades happily took the captives to General Kaito's base camp at Chikung. Later, after dusk, Captain Zhevishe Aye and his party went to the crash site to unload the goods from the plane. They hauled the entire cargo to their foxholes.

The battle had been ensuing for nearly a week by then, and although Naga fighters had surrounded the enemy from every direction, they were somewhat at a loss, for they weren't convinced that going inside the besieged camp was safe. Moreover, they had exhausted their ammo and basically couldn't rush inside barehanded, as it was certain that the enemy would use their last ounce of energy against them.

On August 28, 1960, the daytime was sizzling, and the heat seemed to be taking its toll over the Naga fighters who had been surrounding the camp for days. Impatience was at its peak, and so regardless of the risks involved, they were just about to overrun the camp. Suddenly, two fighter planes appeared on the horizon. In fact, the certainty of appalling casualties on both sides was saved by the bell. The planes started shelling MMG, RPGs, and bombs, randomly inside the bunkers of the Naga guerrillas who were caught unaware. As the Nagas were recovering from the shock of this massive barrage, it offered an opportune moment to the Indian troops. A large number of reinforcements who were waiting outside on the perimeter, barged into the combat zone with the Brigadier on the lead. Thereafter, clusters of other Indian troops from Ukhrul, Meluri and nearby posts, started to gain the upper hand. This left the Naga fighters with no choice other than to leave the site of the besieged camp. Nagas could not accomplish this mission as planned, but this operation delivered extensive damage to the Thuda occupants. They had killed three

Indian soldiers, wounded dozens, fire-bombed the entire barracks; at least two planes were dismantled as well as capturing one with nine crew on board. It was indeed a feat for these great mountain warriors to have brought down planes with bare basic weapons.

In reality, the Nagas had won this battle, because this was the episode that brought this anonymous war to the attention of most of the world. At the insistence of A.Z. Phizo, Gavin Young, a London-based journalist from the prestigious English daily "Sunday times and the Observer," had arrived at Rangoon, Myanmar to observe the war the Nagas wanted to publicise, while Nehru was deliberately trying to hush it up. During those coercion periods, foreign visitors were totally banned from entering the war-torn Hills, lest the visitors may expose the ongoing turmoil to the outside world. Gen. Kaito sent Captain Zhevishe and his team to escort Mr. Young into the war-wrecked region. After Young's arrival, Gen. Kaito dispatched Lt. Gen. Zuheto Swu, Foreign secretary Isak Chishi Swu, and Captain Zhevise Aye, along with 25 soldiers to accompany Gavin Young to the plane crash site. They arrived at the site on March 4, 1961. Mr Young, fit as a stallion, meandered over the place and deftly took pictures of crashed planes and burnt villages. These pictures would afterwards be the factual confirmation that India was truly depriving the Nagas of their universal rights, and the latter had no choice but to put up a tough retaliation. Young took those pictures back to London, and afterwards circulated them in some of the most reputable newspapers in London. Based on this event, Gavin Young also documented the story of "Nagas unknown war" and their struggle for independence; 'the war' which the Indian union would reduce to an internal matter.' The exploits of Gavin Young certainly had a snowball effect in the worlds press back in the 1960s.

General Kaito's brave officers; from left to right Lt. Col Zukiye of Hoshepu, Brigadier Kivihe and Brigadier Ghoshito.

Kaito's soldiers in action.

Seven

The first mission to East Pakistan

Catherine of Sienna wrote, 'To a brave man, good and bad lucks are like his left and right hand. He uses both.' And for us Nagas, we must use both, as shared here...

A dearth of weapons at the arsenal of the Naga army was one of the main obstacles and barriers behind some key battles; the battles, which were then frequently ensuing between the Indian forces and the Naga fighters. Among the hosts of such top examples are the encounter at Hoshepu and the strike at Thuda. Both battles were remarkable, heroic and certainly had their landmark in the journey of Naga arms struggle; however, it had to be called off almost at the climax of its glory owing to the shortage of weapons at their stock. General Kaito could boast of a sizeable loyal army with him but was deterred by lack of guns and ammo, which was the primary basis that urged him desperately to acquire the weapons as soon as possible. But of course, obtaining them would be a walking-on-egg mission, and he needed to weave a careful plan.

Just as General Kaito was setting the means to approach some neighbouring countries for arms aid, the Indian government, too, was rolling up their sleeves to wipe out the Naga fighters. Not only the fighters, but they were also bent on erasing the entire fervour of Nationalism from the Naga culture. Thus, on a daily basis, troops were transported to almost every Naga village and contiguous area of the Naga Hills. It seemed like the whole Naga population could be outnumbered by the strength of Indian troops in the Hills. This led General Kaito to ponder his secret pledge to survive this movement and attain victory, while acknowledging that its goal was visibly limited if he didn't act immediately. The Indian government had also begun to treat Naga people with more disdain than previously. There were times when the Nagas and Indians, along with the Allies, fought side by side on both World War fronts.

By the end of 1961, General Kaito Sukhai had decided to lead his men and venture beyond the border to seek the support of Pakistan. In the past, the Pakistan government had aided the Nagas in some way or another. For instance, when Naga leader AZ. Phizo and some of his associates secretly sneaked into Pakistan to seek their help; it was forthcoming. He was given a safe means of access from Dakha to Karachi, and after his short time lobbying there, Phizo went off to Zurich by acquiring an El-Salvador passport. After that, he went to London. Hence, Kaito believed that Pakistan could be a safe bet and the only potential ally yet. It was also evident to Kaito that India and Pakistan had a rather sour relationship; therefore, the sound reckoning was he wouldn't be turned away by Pakistan when he knocked at her doors. His philosophy "The rival of my enemy is my friend" was to be put to the test and trial.

The two senior leaders Scato Swu, the Khedage and Kughato Sukhai, the Ato Kilonser Federal Government of Nagaland, all but concurred and assented to General Kaito's proposal for a mission to East Pakistan. This was followed by President Scato Swu signing the official letter of approval for the mission. After the coast was cleared, Kaito pitched into the final preparation for the expedition. In the following months, the adept mind of the young General was taken up with skilful selection for the committed fighters among the Naga army. In the spring 1962, General Kaito ordered all the divisional command to send their best soldiers to the mission summit. But apart from some few high-ranking officers, the soldiers were not to be informed about the real intent behind this gathering. This time the plan had to be dealt with deftly and with no loose ends. He didn't want to repeat the same error committed by previous Naga armies who, while boisterously trekking into an operation to East Pakistan, got caught midway. It was unfortunate that the intelligence watchdogs got whiff and captured them while they were still drifting inside the Indian Territory.

Saniba Ao of Chungliyimsen village, Mokukchung, was a graduate, then serving as the Headmaster of Atukuzu Medium English School, Zunheboto. In those days, there were hardly any graduates among the Nagas, and so each time any educated Nagas agreed to deliver his or her service to the FGN, it was regarded as a moment of notable pull-off. Then later, when Saniba Ao received a letter from the top tier of the FGN government, notifying him that his service was required for the Naga National cause, he did not hold back. Not only did Saniba accept the invitation to bond into FGN, but also nobly stated, "If my nation needs my service, why should I shy away from it?" Saniba gladly joined the movement from the day he received the letter.

Saniba Ao was offered a far more vital task on this particular mission about which he was excited. It was not just some sort of ordinary assignment he was called to, but he was to assist General Kaito Sukhai on a red tape errand in this venture. Moreover, how better could it get for young Saniba than being part of a mission where the famed commander-in-chief himself, would be leading a batch of not more than 150 highly principled soldiers inside the rough terrains of East Pakistan to procure war supplies, and learn the art of armed combat. Kaito's fighters were highly excited when informed about the details of their mission, the details of which would come to their notice only on the latter part of the expedition. Nonetheless, it was always the primary obligation of the Naga fighters to observe the mission secrecy at all cost; the component of their mission could not be leaked even to family or loved ones; this mission was no exception. There was never a man so tough as Kaito in enforcing discipline. One day he made his entire elite squad line up and, one by one, kept beating them with a cane. At the end of the line, a man took a beating on his legs but looked Kaito straight in the eyes and said: "Sir, what have I done?" Kaito embraced and kissed the man on his forehead and told the group, "He is the only person here! The rest of you have no feelings; your senses are dead"!

Before departing the Hills, all needful arrangements had been made, and basic provisions had been prepared. Ahead of their coming in, the diplomatic envoys of the FGN were dispatched to Karachi and were in constant touch with the Pakistan Government. Khodao Yanthan, NNC General Secretary, and Yongkong Nganshi Ao, NNC spokesperson, were both stationed in Karachi.

Back at the Hills, frenzied preparation for the mission was secretly going on, Maj. Zhevishe Aye, General Kaito's personal adjutant, was all beck and call to his boss. He had been sent by his chief to a task of arranging military regular in bulk for the selected batch of Naga soldiers. Zhevishe was a brave young officer who had risked his life on numerous occasions and had progressed swiftly to the rank of Major. Subsequently, his bravery and sincerity had also earned him the position of General's Adjutant, a post most of the soldiers would crave. Zhevishe was a native of Sutemi, a village under Zunheboto District. Then, he was engaged to a beautiful young lady and was planning to marry her; however, his nuptial was likely to be delayed for an extended time. As this was a dice with death mission, there was a high chance of him being killed or captured by the enemy, and he might not even return home to see this girl. When she insisted on knowing where and why he was leaving Zhevishe had lied to her. A feeling of guilt rested heavily on this lad's heart as he bade her farewell and trailed pensively towards his headquarters; in fact, protocol forbade him to reveal anything of the mission.

On March 21, 1962, Gen. Kaito took with him around 100 handpicked soldiers from Eastern command and, stealthily as stags, hiked west toward the 5th Brigade Naga Army Base Camp, Zubza River, Niuland Dimapur. Zhevishe also arrived there with a heap of army fatigues, as requested by his chief. Prior to Zhevishe's arrival, General Kaito had sent Capt. Hoito and Lt. Honije of Niqhekhu to survey the routes on which they were set to embark. The two had been sent to scout over an Indian military outpost from the 5th Brigade camp up to the Barak River which falls under Zeliang region; this was the route he would pursue on the first leg of the expedition. Six days later, after careful surveying, the scouting team arrived back at the 5th Brigade Headquarters and informed the finding to General Kaito. After that, they were content to take off.

When everything was set for moving, the chief ordered the purchase of a large pig for slaughter and a departure feast. That evening his soldiers were fed a sumptuous meal. Before leaving the place, Gen. Kaito renamed the 5th Brigade Naga Army Headquarter as 'Total camp.' The next day they moved towards the Zeliang-Naga region, arriving at a village called Shempang, and rested for three days. For the village communities of Shempang, Gen. Kaito's presence on the last day at their village was a day to cherish. It was a brilliant Sunday morning on 8th April. The young leader took a bunch of his jolly officers onto the stage and presented a song called, "Lord I want to be a Christian." It was not every day they got to witness an army General merrily amusing the gathering inside their tiny village church, and as you would have thought, the scene indeed moved the village congregation.

Kaito's soldiers having their dinner before embarking on a gruelling journey.

On April 11, they arrived at Naga army camp, Barak Riverbank. Brig. Daigon Zeliang had established his base there and controlled this region. He greeted his General with delight. They waited for Maj. Gen. Mowu Gwizantsu, GOC Southern Command, who arrived a week later on April 8, with 43 fighters including two female soldiers. After Mowu's arrival with 43 soldiers along with the 107 who were with Gen. Kaito, they then numbered 150. The selected few for this mission wasn't what mattered. Instead, this batch of chosen men should have the tenacity to complete this mission at any cost and return back safely. Of these soldiers, Sümi consisted of 69 soldiers, Angami and Chakesang combined were 43, Lotha 12, Ao 2, Zelaing 12, besides 11 Yimchunger and Sangtams. Following the gathering at Barak River, the command formation was dispersed as follows:

Mission Commander	General Kaito Sukhai
Second Commander	Major General Mowu Gwizantsu
Major General	Hokiye Swu
Quarter Master	Brigadier Tsememo Ovung
Mission Secretary	Major Saniba Ao
Intelligence branch	Inspector Tadingpou Gangmei

From left to right; Major General Hokiye Swu, General Kaito Sukhai, Major General Mowu Gwizantsu and Major Saniba Ao

They were further divided into three companies - Company A under the command of Maj. Khutovi Swu, Company B under Maj. Zhevishe Aye and Company C under Lt. Col Deprale Angami.

Barak River emerges from the Barak ranges Manipur and flows into Surma River in Bangladesh and afterwards meets the Brahmaputra. Finally, it empties into the Bay of Bengal, Indian Ocean. The Nagas marched south of Barak and arrived at a village called Chinkao and headed along Makur River bank till they reached Bolpung village. From Bolpung, they trailed down the Jeri River length. They cautiously avoided the Indian Army outpost at Baladhan, after which they arrived at the bank of Janam River. It was not unusual for Naga fighters to trail the river courses since the riverway was mostly covered with thick forest, providing a perfect camouflage from the vigilant Indian army outposts.

Maj. Zhevishe and Capt. Toshiho, were busy jotting down the entire details of their trips in their diaries. They contained the names of villages they passed through, rivers they swam across, and at least all the bigger hills they had scaled. But most of the soldiers couldn't even keep count of the number of villages they had sojourned or come across; it was the rabbit hole they were plunging into, a never-ending journey to these weary soldiers. To top their gruelling march; sometimes there was a situation when they had to move on empty stomachs for days or more.

Passing through dozens of villages, they arrived at a distinct Kuki community village called Pornapoisa. This village was of concern to General Kaito. Arriving at Pornapoisa village, Kaito unravelled a treacherous deal made by some villager with the Indian Intelligence sleuth named Captain Sethi. On that fateful day in 1959, his trusted and most incisive officer Zhekuto Sema was killed by Indian troops. So enraged was Kaito with Zhekuto's death that he even shed tears of anger. Zhekuto was then serving as the Intelligence Director of Naga National army. On the same occasion, Gen. Thungti Chang of Naga Home Guard was wounded; he was later caught and imprisoned by the Indian forces. The team was returning from Bangladesh, former East Pakistan, after meeting the NNC President A.Z. Phizo, who at the time was lobbying at Karachi. Kaito caught a person named Laukhopau Kuki and one of his accomplices who was to blame for exposing his fellow Naga fighters to the Indian Army. He brought the two Kukis along with him on this trip.

Naga fighters by then were pacing into the steamy forest belt of Maibong Kachari Kingdom, North Cachar hills. They swam across Modhura River and marched to Dohing village. Interestingly, there again at Dohing, Gen. Kaito caught an alleged Indian secret agent who was employed as a clerk at the Deputy Commissioner office in Silchar. Kaito had an ability to outperform his peers in numerous ways; one of them being his amazing ability to read people's minds each time he starts conversing with them. Some way or other, he would pull the strings of the people.

They had stepped into an unfamiliar territory and needed to be extra vigilant, as even sighting by civilians might lead to alerting the Indian troops. They trudged through the clammy forest of Halflong, and marched inside a large conduit of forest belt flanked by Silchar in the east and Jantia hills in the west. In the Death Valley of Silchar and wet jungle of Jantia, they marched. At Silchar, the fighters seized two power wagon jeeps carrying the civilians between the thoroughfares. They emptied the occupants of the jeeps and in their place were loaded the wounded, the weary, and some heavy backpacks they had been dying to drop off. Capt. Hoito and Capt. Jehoto took the wheels of the engines and headed towards the main road. Along with the rest, the civilian passengers were transported through the highway, trailed by the two loaded jeeps. They seldom slept or slouched and slowly drove all through the night. They had travelled quite a distance by dawn, when they slumped down next to a brook which was covered by thick brushwood. Later it was estimated that in that night alone, they travelled for an agonizing 38 miles without a break.

The next night they trudged through Barail reserve forests, combing their way through the twisty liana climbers and had a hard time plucking the blood-sucking leeches off their parched flesh. They swam across the river, clambered through forested hills and then furtively moved towards Old-Nachenjol village. By dawn, they reached the village where General Kaito requested the village elders to leave the injured Tsangtemo and Woshelo in his care. Despite being aware of India's apparent aggression toward Naga army sympathisers, the village elders agreed to keep two injured and look after them.

It was 3 AM in the morning at Detok chara forest, Haflong. Below lay a wide stretch of a plain area with a rail track sited in the middle of an open expanse. Somehow crossing this area could not be avoided; moving to the other side of the hill involved crossing the track. If they avoided going through this open stretch and traversed the other way round, it would be a huge depletion of energy and time. Saving energy and time at this juncture was vital. Then again, what they haven't perceived yet was; the Indian Army by then had got an inkling of their presence in the region, which was why they had jammed all possible roads leading to East Pakistan, as well as this Detok Chara rail track.

The keen eyes of Kaito's scouting party could not sight the rival forces in the proximity, but the enemies were stationed all about the rail station and its adjoining areas. On any given occasion, Naga fighters would travel by nightfall and relax during the daytime. But on this particular night the moonlight was gleaming. They considered that marching overtly into this sort of open terrain would be an unwise decision. Yet, on that occasion, they decided to keep moving under any circumstances so as to progress much more quickly towards their objective. In fact, Kaito was not taking it easy; he had already mulled over the chances that the Indian troops might have received news of his presence in the region, which they had. So, with many speculations at hand, he rushed his men more rapidly.

The night had crept in, and the Indian Armies were placed at every possible entry and exit. They had even boarded the train to use its light, which illuminated the entering corridor like a shimmering stadium. Even the shadows that went beyond this key exit would be obvious. Every measure had been taken to make certain that Nagas would not pass through. Even so, fate combined with Kaito's prudent instinct steered the first two groups slickly across the track. Despite a wide exit lying above, it was their practice of moving under cover of darkness that aided them to exit the railway track below the narrow bridge passage, far from the sight of the Indian Army. Surprisingly, even at that time, the first two groups were not aware of the rival forces that had already secured the area.

To add to their vulnerability, there was also a missing link between the advanced groups and the third group; B Company was still detached at the rear, they approached the covering area where they could clearly sight the rail track and were somewhat at a loss, not clear as to where the first two groups had headed. The bright shaft of light emanating from the crowded train had stopped them from crossing the track. They had not yet discovered the narrow channel through which the first two groups had exited.

The sharp eyes of Company B commander Maj. Zhevishe saw hundreds of Indian forces lurking about the station. It appeared they would be tangled in a major broil had they tried to cross the track. Zhevishe and his men didn't stand a chance for if a gunfight ensued as the shortage of weapons at hand was obvious. Even physically, they were outnumbered, while fatigue was another hurdle. All in all, fighting back at this juncture was not a good idea; running across the track without fighting would evidently expose his group and make them a vulnerable target; Zhevishe was in a quandary. The first two groups had vanished with no idea of the peril that was left behind. The immediate need was to find a way to cross the exit without skirmishing with the rival forces. Despondent and fearful, his mind took some time to clear. Finally, Zhevishe formulated a plan to sneak through alone and locate General Kaito. He was convinced that only his chief could take a sound decision at a time like this. For now, he could not risk his entire Company being slaughtered, so he left them behind and ran towards the crossing; swiftly, he jumped over the beam of light perched across the track and started to look for the trail of his chief; but it was in vain.

Lt. Colonel Zhevishe Aye (now 88 years old) went as a Captain in this trip to East Pakistan

Meanwhile, General Kaito reached the other side of the track with his advancing troops and stopped at Detok Chara village. Shortly after reaching the village, he became very concerned. His intuition caused him to question, "Why is the village so quiet? Why are there no people here? Where is everyone?" The serene silence was rather weird. General Kaito sensed something was not normal, and he had to find out what was going on. Kaito left his soldiers at a secluded place and instructed them to stay calm; while he took with him his Personal Security Officer Capt. Toshiho and intelligence Officer Tadingpou. The trio started to sneak around the village. At the far end some activity was visible. After a while they could sense it was actually a person moving about and they started to follow the person. After a brief chase, they had him surrounded. Kaito asked him why and to where had all the villagers vanished, and why not him. The person reluctantly told him,

"The Indian forces told us to vacate the area as there was a huge war that was going to take place; tonight most probably!" "So, why did you stay back?" The man retorted, "Don't you see, I am an old man and I'm tired of running, so I decided to stay back. Moreover, if I have to die, I don't mind dying here at my village." They took a look at the old man and nodded as if they agreed with him.

The Indian Army had evacuated the villagers during the day and locked down the entire exit. The General was now certain that he had fallen right into the enemy's trap. Perhaps, his only advantage left was the slight possibility of Indian forces not knowing of his triumph over the first obstacle. It may seem slim but it still was an advantage. Just then, the thought of the missing group seized his mind. Swiftly, he called Toshiho and sent him in search of the missing party. He instructed Toshiho to guide them back as soon as he found them so as to join the others.

The situation back at the other side of the track was more threatening; Maj. Zhevishe along with his marooned company was gripped with fear. At any given moment, the Indian Army could pursue and engage them in a fierce exchange of gunfire, which would result in huge loss of lives. Zhevishe prayed that it should not happen. Wasting no time after crossing the track, Zhevishe frantically searched for the other groups; but it was futile. It was getting darker. The moonlight was almost covered with night clouds and visibility was partial. The presence of the enemy did not concern Zhevishe anymore; he was bellowing for help. The more he delayed, the quicker enemies would close in. He considered that uniting with other groups was a priority; pooled together, they could somehow withstand the crisis. Zhevishe started yelling, "ooh! Sir Kaito! Where are you? We are being surrounded! Come and help us!" The shouting continued a few times until Capt Toshiho, not so far away, heard the shrill voice of Maj. Zhevishe. He followed the trail of the voice and soon found sweat-drenched Maj. Zhevishe, tensely hiding at the edge of the narrow path.

Later, Maj. Zhevishe Aye recalled that a fairly audible chanting of 'Namaz' was emanating from the Mosques of the Muslim community residing nearby. Perhaps the enemy mistook his yelling for their chants which is why they did not come chasing after him. Toshiho led the stranded group and funnelled them through the previous narrow passage, finally catching up with General Kaito's group. As for now, they had crossed the primary hurdle but still faced the problem of how to avoid detection by the Indian troops. There was no channel of escape to safety; hundreds of enemy's vigilant eyes were perched in every direction. Also, surrendering and aborting the mission was not an option since they had come this far after and had already gone through so much pain. Gen. Kaito was at the end of himself; not having any military solution.

Kaito had a brief session with his subordinates and then ordered his frustrated soldiers to gather around. He beckoned Head Chaplain Ahokhe Sema and told him, "Let us pray; let us pray to God to deliver us from hands of the enemy." As was tradition, they read out a line from the Book of Psalms chapter 20, verse 7, *"Some trust in chariots, and some in horses, but we will remember the name of the lord."* Then they poured out their hearts. Indeed, after a while heaven answered their prayer in a strange and wonderful way; a complete divine intervention began to take control of the situation. It was indeed an extraordinary phenomenon, recalled by both Major Zhevishe and Captain Toshiho. The moon was bright and the sky was clear blue. Then, suddenly, the atmosphere just above the radius of where the two warring forces were holed up, began to be enveloped in a dark mist. Next was the display in the sky of a sparkling contour, followed by massive rumbling and then an incessant downpour. The ambient light became darker until they could only see each other's faces when lightning struck.

In the meantime, General Kaito conceived a brilliant plan. There were risks involved, but he saw hope in this display of nature's fury.

He directed his soldiers to move towards the forested area. They were to cross the uneven and steep rocky riverbed under the cover of darkness and head through the forest covering. This took the Indian Army by surprise since this was a very inhospitable terrain. It was very uneven and had sheer drops; one wrong footing would mean certain death. And so the enemy would not presume this as an escape route; their attention was focused on other possible openings. Afterwards, his men were amazed; the enemy had them almost by a whisker, and even though this crossing left them exhausted, yet it was the most ingenious plan. The key decision taken at that moment was perfect; Kaito knew it was the only option they could count on at that 'now or never' situation. They signalled to each other, held on to the nearest person's hand and started to move towards the unfriendly riverbed. Meanwhile, the Indian forces had shrunk to cover; an abrupt darkness eclipsing above, combined with the heavy downpour of rain coerced the Indian troops into their burrows, mystified. The Nagas progressed slowly towards the opposite direction of the vicious stony riverbed; they would take a few steps forward and wait until the next flash of lightning. Their stride synchronized with the flash, and this routine continued until they finally crossed the riverbed and pushed inside the forested area. They were safe for the time being. The relief was, however, temporary; in fact there was never time for a break. Regardless of the hammering rainfall, they continued to move forward to the next village. After hours of walking and becoming rain-drenched, they finally arrived at the threshold of Mikikhur village and, of course, all in one piece.

All this while, the civilian passengers of the jeeps were made to trail along with the Naga soldiers. Finally, at the outer-edge of Mikikhur, General Kaito decided to relieve them from the burden of the gruelling walk. He apologised for their trouble but also explained how sending them off in the first place, would have created problems for both parties; the Indian troops would be relentless in finding the trails of Naga soldiers and thus prevent them from leaving the border. Before departing into their separate ways, Kaito gave them a generous sum of money. It was later told that these civilians, after returning, talked highly of the Naga soldiers and extolled them as the real freedom heroes. They had never seen any bunch of fighters who were so starved, broken, weary, but yet so determined.

Weary Naga fighters resting in the wilderness on their way to East Pakistan

At Mikikhur, General Kaito made a headcount and was delighted to know that everyone had survived the terrifying ordeal. He once again gathered his soldiers around, and it was only at that moment Kaito revealed the actual purpose of the mission; he also disclosed the name of the country they were heading to. Until then, most of his officers and the lower ranking soldiers were not informed. His soldiers knew they were onto something crucial, but going to Pakistan for whatever reason, was beyond their comprehension. They were excited with the prospect of going into a foreign land, for a good number of them had never ventured beyond the border. After revealing the purpose of the mission to his soldiers and before continuing on the journey, General Kaito Sukhai gave them the most rousing speech. He said, "Ooohh! Warriors of the Nagas! In this vital mission, your parents, your brothers, your sisters and even your loved ones shall not be with you; it is now yourself, your God and your guns! Thus, keep a big heart, look upon God, rest your fears, and together we will march for the future glory of our Naga Nation."

Sitting down to hear some briefings from the senior officers.

In the past, Naga fighters had gone through countless death-defying missions with this young leader, and never in their ventures had they doubted his judgement. If it was the presence of someone with whom they could rest their fears, it was Kaito. With him, these crude fighters had no dread of risk or obstacles. They envisaged him as the face of hope and conceded to the soundness of his decision; to many of them, he was a demigod. His followers were in awe at the level of his energy. If the mission was precarious, their leader, without slumber, could go on striving for days or even a week, and it never showed it in his eyes. As he would often say, "The plight of my people haunts me even more in my sleep, and sometimes sleeping seems more exhausting than being awake." He would accomplish his mission without a break, and in the end, the results were always encouraging.

Mikikhur village is located on top of a hill, towering above the entire region. Here you could have the perfect vista of a dozen villages speckled around. It has a spectacular view, but a more surprising spectacle awaited them as they came inside the village. The Detok chara residents who had earlier deserted their village were all sheltered here. There was a rumour that these villagers were taking the Indian side. If any of them secretly slipped out, it would be too costly for Kaito and his men, as the villagers would certainly reveal them to the Indian troops. That was why General Kaito thought that the best plan was to get out as quick as they could from the village. Knowing that they would inform the Indian troops about their trail, he cleverly tricked the villagers before they took leave. He told them that they shall be moving to the next village, but firmly warned them not to inform the Indian troops about the plan. After they vanished far from the sight of the villagers, Kaito took a U-turn and went towards the hill just opposite to where he told them he would be heading.

The Naga army marched uphill and rested on a canopy at the summit of a hillock. This place had a perfect vantage point; here, you could have a comfortable view of the adjoining ranges and the plains below. That night they took a rest inside the canopy. The next day was bright and sunny; Kaito crouched down, relaxed, and watched every move of the Indian Army down at the station. Soon, as expected, the villagers indeed tipped-off the Indian soldiers, who went on a wild goose chase. After the Indian troops left, General Kaito marched down hill with his soldiers and went to the same place which the Indian troops had vacated. Standing there, he was laughing up his sleeve, probably pondering how naïvely his rival could be handled. The Indian troops on the other hand would be cursing themselves, wondering how it was even possible for hundreds of men to escape right under their nose, unseen. In fact, they were confounded. Naga fighters by now had moved far north to the course of Surma River, East Pakistan.

Of all the missions they had undertaken, this was by far the most vital and the toughest. The moment Kaito's soldiers learnt where they would be heading, they were possessed with an air of enthusiasm and passion. After about one month travelling, they were now unto the last leg of their journey; approaching the border was just a mile away. Early at dawn on 1st May, they reached the last Indian village called Khaibap Thana. As they advanced towards the village, they saw an old man who appeared to be in his mid-70s, standing outside his hut. It appeared as though he had just woken up after night's sleep. The old man rubbed his eyes, lifted up a water pot and was heading somewhere, seemingly for nature's call. He was totally unaware that hundreds of worn-out eyes were keenly watching his every move. Without further ado, General Kaito slipped out and caught the old man. He asked him, "Where is Surma River?" The old man looked intently into Kaito's face and turned over again to those tattered soldiers who had encircled him. The man was quite perplexed. Kaito persisted with the same question. This time he could observe the gravity in Kaito's eyes, and rather resentfully the old man leered and pointed towards the south of the village. "You come and show us," Kaito ordered. The old man reluctantly took them down some 200 meters below the village and showed them the river. Surma River is the separating line between India and East Pakistan (Bangladesh). Kaito reckoned that crossing the river at any point would mean they would land on Pakistan soil.

Oddly enough, they embarked on their expedition at the tip of Barak River, which turned out to be the tributary which flowed into the Surma River. It was the monsoon season and the Surma River was flooded to an extent. Time and again they grasped hold of each other's hand, since a good number of them could not swim. They were assured that clinging on to each other would form a strong chain which could resist the strong current. The plan worked perfectly, but was hardest on the skilled swimmers among them.

Sited down at the south bend of the river bank, not far from their position, was an Indian army outpost which had by then spotted them. Just about half of them had crossed the river, and the other half were still swathed under the river when the Indian border outpost located some 200 yards down the riverbank, started firing unremittingly at them. To add to the problem, 13 of them were swept away by the river current, but were later rescued unscathed. General Kaito, who was still at the rear, shouted to those who had already landed on the Pakistan side, "Shoot back at the enemy outpost." To those who were still swamped under water, he shrieked, "Drop off all the heavy loads; even your weapons, and move as quickly as you can." He knew that after crossing the river, their old weapons would be of no use, since they would have landed into a friendly zone. Just then, Toshiho, who was already on the Pakistani side, had spotted the positions where the enemy had been hitting out. Despite his short build, Toshiho lifted up the bulky LMG on his shoulder and shelled incessantly towards the Indian position. All attention was now on him with the rival forces starting to hit back at his position. This diversion allowed those who were still submerged under the river to have a narrow escape. Overall, it was one last attempt to forestall the Nagas from crossing the border, which had failed. Instead of holding them back, they got a befitting reprisal from the Naga army. Moments after stepping onto Pakistani soil with his last unit of soldiers, General Kaito ordered them to spend their remaining bullets and mortar shells, firing towards the Indian camp.

Toshiho Naga (now 86 years old) former Personal Security Officer of General Kaito who also went as a Captain on this Trip to East Pakistan

What added more light to their euphoric moment was an interesting incident that followed. Shortly after landing inside the friendly zone in Pakistan, the Naga fighters saw a lone Pakistani guy coming towards them. The man was shouting in Hindi, "Idhar nahin, udhar maro," his finger pointing towards the Indian side. He was yelling at the Naga soldiers to fire at the position where the Indians were positioned and from where they were shooting. While the guy approached, Maj. Gen. Hokiye, to make certain they had landed at the right place, queried the person in Hindi. "Yeh zamin kiska hain, India ka hain ya Pakistan ka." ("Is this Indian soil or Pakistan soil?") The man responded, saying, "Yeh zamin Pakistani ka hain." ("This is Pakistan.") General Kaito beamed and asked him, "Tum fire karoge"? ("Will you fire at the Indians"?) The man nodded back in affirmation. Kaito then handed over the gun to him; without any glitch, the person loaded the gun and started firing gaily towards the Indian outpost. The Naga soldiers watched him, thrilled. Later it was learnt that the person was a regular Pakistani soldier who was on leave.

As reported on the radio afterwards, it was learnt that there was a huge number of casualties on the Indian side, but fortunately, none of the Nagas was killed or hurt. At an award ceremony, Maj. Toshiho Naga, along with Brigadier Tsemomo Ovung and Jehoto Sümi, were feted for their bravery by General Kaito. Later, back at home, Toshiho was henceforth nicknamed as "Toshiho the faster gun" for his courageous act, which indeed had averted an impending tragedy on the river.

It was May 1, 1962, when they stepped into the suburbs of Sylhet, an East Pakistan city flanked by the Indian border in the Northeast. It was a moment of success and jubilation for the Naga fighters. After a month-long journey, trekking thousands of miles, combing thick jungles, straggling through harsh ravines and dodging dozens of vigilant enemy security outposts, they finally walked into East Pakistan. It truly required nerves of steel to accomplish a mission such as this. And what will leave present-day military commanders bemused with questions is: General Kaito defied all the sophisticated amenities such as compasses, visual aids and paraphernalia of basic military facilities to fulfil this mission. It took him just a grubby map drawn on a piece of paper and set with his sheer instinct and full conviction to rip into one of the most fortified frontiers in the world, with 148 of his strong-willed soldiers. Out of 150 Naga soldiers, 148 arrived safe and sound, with the exception of two injured soldiers, Tsangtemo and Woshelo, who were left behind at old Nachanjol village. They brought along with them three Indian spies who were caught on the way, and were later handed over to the Pakistan army.

Nagas heaved a sigh of relief after reaching Sylhet. The pain of the journey was bitter, but the result was noteworthy knowing that the cause was worthwhile. Through the streets, they ambled peacefully yet clumsily, and the residents gazed at them like some new entrants on a show; their clothes tattered, hair dishevelled, their faces tired and drained. It appeared as if they had just emerged from the clutches of some monsters in a thrilling Hollywood movie. And in some way, it was true! For they had indeed prevailed over the similar sorts of threats. Although gazed upon with strange looks, some of the residents greeted them with kind gestures. Naga soldiers to them resembled more of a friend in need of help rather than the aggressors. The officer in charge of the Pakistani army arrived and restricted them from hanging about a location. They were kept in military formation and were told to shred all their belongings, including their frayed garments. A short time later, an Army Major accompanied by the district administrator arrived to greet them. The Pakistan army accorded them a warm reception and they were fed a sumptuous meal. After carrying out a battery of protocols, they were taken to an isolated educational institute called Khademnagar Medical College. The medical students were on recurring holiday and the building was vacant for the time being. The surroundings were fairly pleasant and straight away they liked the place.

As a temporary measure, Naga soldiers were told to remain within the confines of Khadem Nagar Medical College Sylhet. One good outcome that happened during their one month stay at Khadem Nagar, was that the soldiers who weren't used to being confined, didn't want to just squander their time either. They kept their timetable ticking with physical exercises and voluntary Hindi speaking classes, which was taught among themselves. Nagas, in any case, would not remain idle. After all, they had been through enough sacrifices to arrive there. They were here to improve themselves and become a lethal fighting force to be reckoned with. The zeal to become proficient more rapidly against their enemy, was prevailing even at the origin of their struggle. Nagas, in comparison to India, were insignificant in the eyes of that nation. Yet, set with courage and the zeal of acquiring back their intrinsic rights, their hopes were growing much stronger all the time. The propagation preached by leaders such as Kaito, Phizo and others were becoming visible; the seeds had been sown by their predecessors some three decades back when the Naga Club submitted the memorandum to the Simon Commission on January 10, 1929. Now the seeds have sprouted. Men like Phizo, Kughato, Scato, Kaito, Mowu, Khodao, Yonkong, Isak, Muivah, Khaplang and thousands of other Nagas after them, have been handed down the task of carrying on the Naga Club legacy, "for tomorrows future, if not today," the seeds must someday be developed into a budding plant.

On 9th August 1962, Pakistan Army Maj. General arrived from the Headquarters. The order had been passed to relocate the Naga fighters from Sylhet to Dhaka. The time had finally arrived for them to begin a realistic military exercise under the funding of the Pakistani Army. The thrilled fighters were taken from Sylhet and flown to Dhaka. Everything was done stealthily; after reaching Dhaka they were not even allowed to step on the ground, perhaps for security reasons. They were boarded directly into an army truck bound for unnamed outskirts of Dhaka, and thereafter, the training commenced.

General Kaito, Phizo and the other officials at East Pakistan 1962.

Eight

The London escapade

On 18th May 1962, NNC spokesperson Yonkong Ao arrived from Dhaka accompanied by a Pakistani Army Brigadier and a Captain. The two Pakistani officers greeted General Kaito Sukhai with high esteem; perhaps, they already had heard of this man's reputation back in India. This five-and-a-half-foot gentleman had hundreds of brilliant battles under his belt and, of course, the most dreaded and widely hunted individual to the entire fleet of sub-continental army. There was a price on the head of many, but Kaito topped the list followed by his trusted Lieutenant Zukiye of Hoshepu, another hell raiser to the Indian troops. It was an open secret then that anyone who got this young General 'dead or alive' would earn himself the 'Maha Vir Chakra', a medal any Indian soldier would covet. The Pakistani officers had a firm handshake with General Kaito and gave a momentary look at his gleaming face; they replied with the same warmth and sat down together musingly. After settling in, they went into a lengthy discussion over matters relating to the long list the young General was seeking in aid from the Pakistan Government. The Government Envoys assented to his demands, and the outcome was fairly positive. Yonkong and the two Pakistani officials left General Kaito and went back to Dhaka.

Yonkong arrived again a week later on May 25. This time he brought an important guest with him, Mr. G.N. Patterson from Great Britain. He was the founding Director of the International Committee for the

Group Rights Study. Patterson had come along with Yonkong to take note from Kaito about the plight that had gripped the Naga people ever since the origin of this war, and the volume of brutality accounted to his people. After listening to those distressing and appalling tales of the Nagas, Patterson went back to London, somewhat saddened.

A.Z. Phizo, the NNC chief who was based in London, had been kept well informed with regard to the situation developing at the domestic turf; he was constantly fetching the correspondence through the diplomatic pouch of a third country. Phizo, having received the news of Kaito and his troops landing safely into the Pakistan base, now started cautioning New-Delhi of the consequences through several press hand-outs to the British press. By the end of May, Phizo air-dashed to Karachi to patch up policies with Kaito and others.

On 3rd June 1962, General Kaito flew to Karachi with his secretary Saniba, to coordinate with Phizo. Kaito stayed in Karachi while Saniba was sent back to Sylhet on 11th June. After staying for nearly a fortnight in Karachi, Phizo left for London on the second week of June. Phizo invited Kaito and Mowu to see him in London so that they could jointly address the issues of the Naga Independence Movement to the English press. On 12th June, Kaito called upon Mowu, Hokiye and Tadingpou to meet him at Karachi. General Kaito informed his officers that he and Mowu would be leaving London for a while, and so he apprised Hokiye and Tadingpou on what should be done during their absence. Accordingly, Mowu stayed back with Kaito at Karachi, while on 20th June, Gen. Hokiye and Inspector Tadingpou were told to go back to the Naga soldiers stationed at Sylhet.

Kaito, Mowu, Khodao and Yonkong left for London from Karachi on September 10, 1962, with their papers forged as Pakistan Nationals. They were, however, detained at the immigration section at Heathrow airport since the passport on which they were travelling was considered incriminating by the Immigration officers.

London times report, September 12, 1962: A Home office statement said *"four persons describing themselves as Nagas refused leave to land at London airport yesterday because the documents on which they were travelling did not satisfy Immigration as to their identity and their nationality."*

David Astor entered the scene. David was an editor of the prestigious English tabloid, Sunday Times and The Observer. He was born to a wealthy American family and raised in the opulence of a great country estate where the political and intellectual elites gathered. However, his compassion for the poor was far beyond any other concern of his; he would always facilitate the victims of political dysfunction. During South African unrest, he voiced a strong opposition to the apartheid policy of the white South African Government and supported "The African National Congress." He also campaigned for Nelson Mandela's release.

Nagas, at this point in time, did not have many connections in the international scene. However, David and Patterson were among the few key links that the Nagas had been betting on in her pursuit of liberation from the forced Indian union. Two years earlier, at the insistence of Phizo, David Astor covertly sent one of his vibrant reporters, Gavin Young to the war-ravaged Naga Hills, to gain insight on the ensuing reality of the conflict; the conflict which the Indian Government was basically trying to veil-off from external eyes.

As soon as he learned about the news of four Naga leaders being detained at Heathrow airport, David called in an attorney, Louis Blom-Cooper, from a top British firm of lawyers. He told Cooper that the Naga leaders were there to present their case through the British press, and that these leaders needed to be released by any means. After the intervention of Blom-Cooper, they were released on the ground of being commonwealth subjects. The British Government was well informed that the Nagas have every reason to object to the arbitrary inclusion of their Hills into the Indian domain. Further, segregating their land between two international precincts of India and Myanmar was deceitful and not for the good of their people. However, the Britishers have long washed their hands, for they do not want to rescind the past, as it will unknot dozens of pertinent burdens that they had already wrapped up. Secondly, even if Great Britain had some sympathy for the Nagas, she certainly does not wish to annoy economy generating giants like commonwealth India. Such was the basis for Britain's silence on this relevant issue.

The release of Kaito and the other three was truly a sight for sore eyes; it was marked with grand delight. Patterson, Phizo, David Astor and his staff, along with throngs of Naga sympathisers, arrived at Heathrow airport to celebrate and greet the four Naga leaders. The four arrived elegantly clad in western outfits and were greeted at the gates by the residents with a bouquet of flowers. They made a good impression; Kaito, slim with striking Mongolian features; Mowu, tall, ruggedly handsome and looking more an athlete than a guerrilla commander; Yonkong, a charming young diplomat, Khodao, polite and commanding fluent English.

The four were buzzed around by an army of reporters. Naga leaders were somewhat taken by the warm reception they were given at London. It had been only a few months since arriving safely in Pakistan and then successively to London. They couldn't ask for more. They chewed the cud over it and thought that at this rate, solving the Naga issue was only a stride away. Reporters were more captivated and smitten by the presence of General Kaito Sukhai amidst them, since they believed him to be the world's youngest General. Well, it was right. Many reviewers and reporters were of the opinion that even at the age of 29, Kaito was probably the world's youngest Commander-in-chief. For the record, he was officially appointed as the Commander-in-chief of the Naga National Army by the Federal Government of Nagaland on the 22nd March 1956, at the age of 23. Kaito's appointment to the post of Commander-in-chief and receiving the label 'World's Youngest General' cannot be put down to sheer circumstance or due providence. In fact, there are many able leaders, including the competent old-hand, Thungthi Chang, the Chief of another powerful Naga rebellion group called the Naga Home Guards. Thungthi was much favoured by the NNC Chief over young Kaito; however, this young Safe Guard Chief whose valour and radiance had well navigated past his age and time, won over the golden opinion of Naga people, and thus they opted for him over other heavyweights to be the person in charge of the newly founded Naga National Army.

With hope against hope, this young General had systematically prepared his Army in whatever skimpy means he could manage and was, of course, leading a fleet of jungle-hardened tribal soldiers, fighting against the colossal empire of India, a Nation relatively fifty times much larger in area and hundred times more superior in military or population count. The number of Naga fighters could be very much lesser, but 40,000 was what the British reporters were informed regarding the size of Kaito's army at that time. Leaving aside the numbers, literally, these were the fighters who were conceived and matured in the shades of war, and they were no stranger to warfare and killings, as to fear and pain.

The twentieth century had seen many great revolutionaries. They fought and won their struggles by different approaches. For instance, a non-violence champion like Gandhi, and anti-apartheid hero, Nelson Mandela, were the ones who fought more diplomatically and had liberated their people by peaceful means. With the same magnitude, Leaders like TE Lawrence, Mao Zedong, Fidel Castro, Gen. VO Nguyen Giap, Michael Collins, Che Guevara, etc. fought with a military approach and won with means of different tendency. They were also the top genius of guerrilla fighters, and yet the dark side of the majority of them were left untold, they consent to wanton massacre, rape and torture to many of their own people while trying to justify their actions.

General Kaito Sukhai was not just a genius and fearless in the art of guerrilla warfare, he was a protector of his people. Anyone who was found mistreating another was punished. With his style of leadership and love for people he truly preceded all the factors if not more than those listed.

It could also be said that in the art of guerrilla warfare, Kaito could be the prime even in comparison with the notable guerrilla fighter Che Guevara, because Kaito was just about 17 years old when he first banded his private militia to defend his tribesmen from the Indian suppression. In fact, Kaito and Che's, struggles had a similar rendering in a way. They were of the same generation; both were young, and their prominence in the style of guerrilla warfare was spellbinding and although, Kaito wasn't reared like Che academically, but the level of intelligence, stratagem and fanatical principles were equally incredible. Desires for wealth Kaito had none; he shunned luxury and led a Spartan existence. Unifying his race and the oppressed into an ordinary's people nation was his obsession.

In contrast to the receptive welcome accorded to Kaito, Mowu, Khodao and Yonkong, Great Britain was uninterested regarding Phizo's arrival years ago. They were conscious of Phizo's link with the Japanese during WWII; hence, Phizo's presence in London did not evoke such a genial sight, which was why his stay in London was not buttressing much merit either. At the same time Phizo was also of the view that his two young dynamic commanders, Kaito and Mowu, could distinctly present the Naga story in a crystal-clear picture, because back in their homeland, these two leaders were practically involved in the day-to-day no-nonsense fight against the intimidating Indian troops and had lived through the sufferings. The main motive of the duos arrival in London was also to present the Naga issue through the British press.

Phizo turned up at the airport with Patterson and received them at the reception. Their stay in London was sponsored by Patterson and his organisation known as the International Committee for Group Rights Study. Over dinner, at Patterson's place, Mowu shared the account of adventures and trouble which they encountered during their passage to Pakistan and then to London. This mission was the first of its kind. Never before had any other Naga freedom fighters attempted or achieved such a complex mission. Patterson and Phizo were truly awed with the passion and courage of these two young leaders. They also had a lengthy deliberation over what must be done during their stay in London.

The Daily Herald (UK, London) Thursday 13th September, 1962. "At 29 he is probably the youngest Army C-in-C in the world."

Their march voted for freedom by Peter Moorhead (The daily Herald September 13, 1962).

The sad-faced little man walked alone across London's Clapham Common. No-one recognised General Kaito, the fearless commander-in-chief of the 40,000- strong Naga rebel fighters from a remote country once notorious for its head-hunters.

But his face is imprinted in the minds of 40,000 battle-hardened Indian troops with orders to "shoot him on sight" as the "Forgotten" war of the commonwealth enters its seventh year on India's northeast frontier.

At 29, he is probably the youngest Army C-in-C in the world, but in his light blue, lightweight suit he looked more like a diplomat than the hero of a hundred fights.

His handshake was warm but firm, his smile friendly, but his eyes were sad and far away, thinking perhaps, of those 500 miles walk he had to take to plead his case for freedom before the United Nations.

Indian House in London was alerted, and unsurprisingly, the Indian consulate in London had alerted New Delhi too. Kaito was invited by the British media to address a press conference on the issue of the Naga Independence Movement. On this occasion, he delivered a moving speech on how back home, his people were concentrated in thousands like animals just because they wanted India to leave them as they were. This address of Kaito was the quantum leap in the journey of the Naga struggle. Thus far, most parts of the world were not even aware that Naga Hills existed, or of the war these tribal inhabitants had been silently waging against India for almost a decade. Interestingly, Gen. Kaito was invited by the British Military strategists to deliver a basic theory on guerrilla fighting tactics. They were completely awed by the level of proficiency this young leader possessed. Kaito was remarkable in the shooting event; the British soldiers were not expecting that this five and a half footed tribal General could outrank the best marksmen among the British officers, but this daredevil did so. As a token of admiration, the officers rewarded him a splendid binocular, which he later gave away to his partner Zukiye Zhimomi. Time and again, Kaito was singled out for interviews by the British army. The Veterans of the Burma War associations also invited Kaito and others on one occasion; among them was Khodao Yanthan, who had been formerly conferred the Burma star. The veterans welcomed them with delight and appreciation. The association expressed gratitude towards the Nagas for their valuable services to the Allies in the Burmese Campaign. On this event General Kaito was honoured by the Burma star association.

At that time, if there was any British subject who had more familiarity and a strong bond with the Naga community, it would be none other than Ursula Betts, a. k. a Ursula Graham Bower. Of course, there were a number of British subjects in the likes of Professor J.H. Hutton, J.P Mills, Sir Charles Ridely Pawsey and many others who had recently returned after their brief stint in the Naga Hills, either as an administrator or anthropologist; but Ursula's name stands tall among them. She had a strong connection with Naga fighters as Ursula herself had led a band of Naga fighters, the "Watch and Ward" force, against the Japanese imperial army in the Burmese campaign. She had also written a book on Naga tribes, 'The Naga Path' and 'The Hidden Hills.' Ursula was appointed to the rank of Captain during WWII. In those days, a female serving in the British Army was quite uncommon; however, it was not surprising in the case of Ursula. She was nothing like any other average woman her age; she had resilience and an exemplary courage to be reckoned with. Her origination from the lineage of a military family was another fixation that urged her to be infatuated with combating skills. She apparently learned to use guns at the age of 12. After being chosen as the leader of V force, more popularly known as Bower-force - 'a scouting patrol party.' Many RAF pilots owed their lives to her. In many instances, they were dragged away into the thick jungles and brought to the Naga tribe's safe hands after crashing their plane. As a matter of fact, Ursula had even decided what exactly should be done if she ever was in danger of falling into Japanese hands. She would shoot herself; while her faithful servant Namkai was instructed to chop off her head and present it to the Samurais as proof that she was dead, to avoid the enemy torturing local Naga people in an attempt to discover her whereabouts.

Leaving her remarkable footprints among the section of Naga people, Ursula Betts had returned from Northeast India some years back. On her initial visit to the Hills, so charmed was she by the beauty of natural landscapes and the camaraderie of affable people dwelling there that even after her exit to Scotland, she would constantly ruminate over the comradeship she had with these tribal people. When she first arrived in the Naga Hills, she stayed with the Tangkhuls Nagas, a short span with the Rongmei Nagas, and then a lengthy period with the Zeme Nagas. Ursula was pet-named the 'Naga queen' by some Naga tribes; there was also an American comic strip titled 'the jungle queen' based on her role during the war in Burma.

David Astor requested Ursula's presence in London as he wanted to gain more insights on Naga people and their struggle. Ursula, then on her late 40s, was somewhat unique in appearance from other women; her fashionable form of boyish trimmed hairdo and donned in a manlike outfit, she nevertheless looked classy and beautiful. She came all the way from Scotland to meet David Astor and the Nagas at London. After meeting them, she took the four Nagas to her private estate at Scotland for a holiday. "I am proud to have them as my guest," Ursula said. The two Naga leaders General Kaito Sukhai and Major Gen. Mowu Gwizantsu, were able to wear their army uniforms for the first time in Britain because they were on private property. The British Government does not recognise their Army.

They had a short sojourn at the farm house of Ursula Betts and her husband Lt. Col. Nicolson Betts, which was located on the 'Isle of Mull'. They spent the day cleaning rifles in preparation for a hunting expedition that Betts had arranged for them. "The only thing that disappoints us is that there are no tigers here," said their spokesman, Mr. Yongkong. The hunting episode was filmed by the Scottish TV and was aired from a station in London; the main idea of the film was to bring to highlight the Naga skill with weapons as well as the war they had been raging against the powerful force. Fortunately, it was the mating season of Sāmbhar deer, and so Lt Col. Betts took them on a hunting spree. In the event, Kaito shot a large stag with a fine set of antlers. That kill made the day. Indeed, Kaito being a skilful hunter, had plenty of stories about his hunting skills and his reflexes in handling guns. But a more outstanding one was recalled by Lt. Col Zhevishe Aye of Naga Army. On one of the expeditions to their HQ in Myanmar border, it so happened that they spotted a pack of scattered wild boars, running disorderly behind thick hedges on marshy slopes. Even as others were in a state of confusion; Kaito took up his rifle and started firing into what appeared to be more like an empty space. His soldiers were not certain what he was shooting at. They thought their General was carelessly shooting at the bushes. However, to their utter surprise, Kaito had shot five boars. Zhevishe still marvels, "It was out of the ordinary! Yet unmistakable; logically no normal human eyes could capture the swiftness of those pack of wild animals, but yet he did; he was truly gifted."

Kaito with his kill (Sāmbhar deer) at the Isle of Mull, Scotland.

Ursula took the four Nagas and travelled down to see her daughters at the hostel about 200 kilometres away from her house. More often, Ursula used to recount all the zesty tales about the Nagas and their extraordinary way of living to her two young daughters. Her girls, she guessed, would be delighted to meet them. Indeed, Trina and Allison were excited when they met the four Nagas. Trina, at the time just eleven years old, remembers how fancy her mother, Gen. Kaito, and the other three arrived at her hostel that wonderful evening. Kaito brought for the girls a large portion of deer's meat he had shot during the hunt. In Sümi Naga custom, the meat of hunted wild animals was usually presented to relatives and close friends as a mark of reverence and a sharing of blessing. At dinner, 20 or so girls of Trina and Allison's boarding house relished on the delectable deer's meat.

The Nagas had a great time with Highlanders. Ursula took them out to the countryside for sightseeing. Also, she would often take them out individually on a stroll, to learn about their feelings towards each other. Later on, she would tell her daughters about the characters of each of the four Naga guests; Mowu, sincere yet austere and not easy to talk with, and Kaito, jovial and happy-go-lucky. Of all the four, Ursula had a profound fondness for Kaito. She described him as a gifted individual with a pleasant outlook. Being a guerrilla commander herself, she understood well the trades of this young General, and, therefore, had an extra admiration for him. On the other hand, Ursula couldn't have an amiable connection with Phizo.

Her disparity with Phizo was largely attributed to T. Sakhire's killing six years previously. Ursula admired Sakhire a lot, and she would define him as a talented publicist. As much as she loved the Nagas, she was more upset over the tragic death of an educated and gifted Naga individual like Sakhire. But despite her critical feelings towards Phizo, Ursula never mentioned this to David Astor, for fear it may damage the relationship between the Nagas and David.

Ursula Betts sightseeing with General Kaito, Mowu, Khodao and Yonkong in Scotland (the two Naga Generals could wear their full uniform in Britain because they are in a private estate, Great Britain did not recognise their Nationhood).

T. Sakhire and Kaito were paradoxically related in some way; they were among the few Naga revolutionaries who could voice their opinion openly against the imposing decisions of their elder leader, Phizo. Sakhire was vocal about taking up arms at the beginning of the movement, but despite of his indignation with the suppression by the Indian Government, he would later favour a more peaceful approach. Kaito, by contrast, was of a strong view that India could not be moved by diplomatic procedures alone; and hence, militarism should flow jointly with diplomacy. But it was only later that Kaito started losing his grip on the opinionated policy of the NNC leader, and decided to improve his own path. He became less favourable towards Phizo's diplomatic viewpoints, considering him as having no political relevance. Even Mowu agreed with Kaito on the matter.

For young leaders like Kaito and Mowu, the burdens back at home had weighed heavily upon them. However, they had been tirelessly shouldering it with the hope that Phizo would be raising the sails of the Naga struggle in the exterior realm. But the instant they arrived in London and examined the vulnerable conditions of their leader, the duo were proved wrong. The pair envisioned that the Nagas' struggle was on the verge of decline if it had to depend on the external context. It is unfortunate that Phizo didn't hold much influence in the western community; he was rather tangled into a susceptible state. Kaito was dismayed, and at the same time incensed, with Phizo's position, and thus, he had a split hairs argument with his leader - "You're doing nothing noteworthy; while back home, the score of us have been left high and dry with our back against the wall." After Kaito returned to Naga Hills, he gallingly questioned Phizo's leadership to the FGN leaders.

General Kaito briefing maps at London.

Nine

Homeland here we come

Khodao and Yonkong stayed back in London with Phizo, and they went on to settle there; Yonkong till his death, while Khodao married an English wife and lived there, although they separated later. Strangely, London became their Alcatraz for the next three decades, and they did not return to Naga Hills until the death of A.Z Phizo in 1990. After the death of the NNC President, Khodao split away from the NNC and founded his own group, the NNC Non-Accordist.

Gen. Kaito and Gen. Mowu, after almost four month's in Britain, returned to East Pakistan on the chilly winter evening of 17th December, 1963. Straight away, they went to visit their boys at Urra - a military training site renamed by the Kaito's boys at Dhaka.

It was 27th December 1962, and 147 pairs of glossy black leather boots clacked together and rested standstill in formation at the training ground of Urra camp, western Dhaka. The vibes were lively and promising as General Kaito Sukhai, with a cane rod clutched in his hand and an olive beret hat tucked under his arms, regally entered the parade ground that cold winter morning. The mood of the Naga- fighters convening with their Chief after wrapping up their training for a minute, seemed like the students getting together with their parents after a graduation. They couldn't hide their delight. In a matter of just eight months stay, the rudimentary jungle warriors had been transformed into refined soldiers, a hybrid of wild and sophisticated, which made them more lethal. Given the quality of the training they had undergone, and with the passion they possessed, it seemed like they were ready to tackle any class of world military if only numbers were not to be taken into account. General Kaito congratulated his soldiers and stated rather humorously yet with severe intention, "Comrades! The time has arrived for us to return to our homeland and settle some scores."

Naga fighters had stayed in East Pakistan for nearly eight months. During that time, they had an extensive military exercising course where enough warfare skills, as well as scores of sophisticated weapon-handling techniques, were amassed. The good news was that the Pakistan army was more than willing to provide all the war supplies they could muster; the bad news was they had to carry the entire supply on their back all the way across the border. Earlier, talks had transpired between the Pakistani officials and General Kaito, over the matter of hauling the weapon supplies to some distinct Naga territory by military planes. But the problem was, Nagas did not have a suitable air-strip yet, and so the option was disregarded.

On the 10th January 1963, Naga fighters bid adieu to their training den on the outskirts of Dhaka; they were taken out on army mobile trucks bound for Dhaka city. For some inevitable security protocols, Nagas were stranded at the airport for about a day or two. However, on 12th January, they were boarded on two planes and flown down to Chittagong. The returning course would be different this time. Even though they would be trekking through a vast length of Myanmar's territory, the risks would be fewer in contrast to the old Cachar route, where the maximum number of Indian troops had been deployed. They were flown straight down to Chittagong, the south of Bangladesh, and from Chittagong, they planned to leap into Burma, and thereafter would sneak into Northeast India from the west Burmese[4] border.

---
4 Myanmar

On the 16th January 1963, Colonel Khan of the Pakistan Army, took lead of a dozen military motorboats, with the entire Naga soldiers onboard, and propelled down to Songo River. They finally came ashore at Dhansi post; apparently, the last Pakistan military post located at the south end of Songo river bank. Colonel Khan and his team bade farewell to Nagas at the border; he also gave away his faithful dog to go along with the Nagas. Aside from all the weapon supplies they had rendered to the Nagas, Colonel Khan also gave a substantial sum of money to General Kaito on behalf of the Pakistan military.

In fact, given the circumstances of having to pass through the mean courses of the vast, rugged and damp Burmese hills on foot with about 50 to 90 pounds of metals on their back, would be a feat next to impossible. It seemed courage and conviction alone would not suffice; they would also need a great deal of energy to sustain through these great obstacles. And so it was thoughtful of the Pakistan Army to devise a meticulous plan to help the Nagas make it through with their food unspoiled, and energy conserved. They issued energy-rich, long-lasting food such as soybean biscuits, hardened bean chunks, nuts and dried-up meat, to help the Nagas make it through without depleting their energy.

Few among them had mastered the art of map reading. So, unlike their arrival from the North Cachar passage, their navigation out of these unfamiliar Burmese terrains was not so much of an issue now. The main hindrance would be the heavy loads of war supplies, and how to navigate the Naga Hills. Depending on their physique, these loads ranging from 50 to 90 pounds were divided. There was no distinction; even their commander-in-chief was no exception. From low-ranking soldier to the highest-ranking officer, weapon stacks were evenly divided, and thus set with belief and a greater devotion to their cause; they embarked on a perilous bone-breaking life-risking journey homeward.

On 21st January 1963, Nagas stepped onto Burmese territory. Apart from the bulky load, the swollen legs and the ravenous belly, they had to be prepared for ambush anytime, for they were stamping on Burmese toes unannounced. A safe passage was never guaranteed. After three days of trekking, they marched wearily into the Shenku region. In the late afternoon, they settled on the bank of Kaladhan River. It required a careful preparation to cross this outsized river; therefore they decided to rest by the river bank and were setting up the means to cross it in the morning. Fortune has it, the next day, the Burmese commuter boat was passing through that way, and General Kaito requested the owner of the boat to ferry them across the river and then offered him some money, but the owner insisted to ferry them free of charge. After crossing the river they hiked to Shetlow village and rested there. The same day a Naga soldier named Henizhe Sema of Kivikhu village went missing in the wilderness. Ironically, he did return to Nagaland, but sadly, it was after spending fifteen arduous years in a Burmese jail. Like many of the early Naga freedom fighters, his was also a forgotten account. By the time he returned to his village in 1978, he was already an old man. He died unmarried sometime back in 2010; such is the bygone fate of some of the early Naga freedom fighters.

By Friday 1st February 1963, after weeks of straggling into thick jungles, steep canyons, and ruthless ravines with bone-breaking metal-stack on their backs, they wearily drew close to a Chin village called Luntang. As Naga guerrillas came into the village, they came upon a swarm of people. It was learned that Chin Hills Baptist Association was hosting an annual congregation at Luntang. General Kaito met the Chin leaders and introduced himself as the commander of the Indian Army and he was patrolling with his soldiers to comb out the Naga guerrillas in the region. Judging by the skin textures and physical build, it didn't convince the Chin people that these soldiers were indeed Indians. They knew the Indians would be taller and a whole lot darker, but what got the Chins, it seemed, was the garments.

Nagas were clad in what was more matching to Indian military fatigue. Later, when their allegiance was tested, General Kaito revealed his real identity to Chins; he told them, "We are Naga freedom fighters, returning home after our training in East Pakistan." Given the fact that Nagas were their nearest cousin, the Chins were indeed delighted to host them. They said, "We feel proud to know about what Nagas were up to." Great feasts were prepared for the Naga fighters, and extra rations were provided to them for their onward journey.

Anonymous and mischievous as Kaito was, he usually never revealed his genuine identity unless their allegiance was tested. In another similar incident, one fine day in December 1966, a group of people came to meet him while he was stationed at Charang, in Assam state. The group was an Assamese resistance group; in effect, they were preparing to launch a revolutionary movement in Assam. Apparently, their resistance movement was stirred by the Naga revolutionaries. As interesting as it gets, at the entrance, the sentries manning the gates, asked the Assamese group about the reason for their visit. They said, "We have come to meet a person named General Kaito Sukhai." It so happened that they had heard a lot about this young General, but seemingly had not met him in person. After a while, the sentries went to General Kaito and informed him about the visiting guests. General Kaito disguised himself as a secretary and went to meet the group. He told them if only they could tell him the purpose of meeting, he would apprise his General on the matter and maybe he would want to see them. The Assamese group hence, informed him exactly why they wanted to meet the General. Thereafter, Kaito returned to his office and sent his guard to invite them to his office. When the Assamese group came into his office and saw that General Kaito was none other than the same secretary whom they had talked with in the first place. They were confused as well as amused. Such was the rareness of this man. Perhaps if the Assamese group had not come to him on good terms, he would have turned them away at the first instance.

Nagas spent the night at Luntang village and in the morning a guide, an ex-serviceman from Luntang, was arranged to escort the Naga fighters out of the Burmese territory. By 6th March, Naga fighters reached Herinkot, a Burmese Naga village. The news of General Kaito's return had by then reached the villagers; the villagers had prepared a wonderful reception to welcome the General and his soldiers. It was truly a heart-warming sight; villagers had decorated their surroundings and cleaned their homes to give a welcoming spectacle to the returning heroes. A grand feast was prepared by slaughtering a large pig, and the fighters were fed to the brim upon their arrival. Finally on 11th March 1963, the Naga Army reached their 1st Divisional headquarters at Thewati-Chikung Mountains, adjoining the Burmese border.

The expedition to East Pakistan was another stepping stone for the rise of the Naga National Movement. Subsequent to General Kaito's return from East Pakistan, Nagas had found a way to deal with the issue of arms shortage. The Naga Army started sending thousands of fighters to haul in weapons and obtain training from the Pakistan army. The next batch comprising of about 1,000 soldiers under the command of Lt. Gen. Zuheto Swu, who went to Pakistan and returned with tons of weapon supplies. This was followed by similar expeditions of two more batches going to Pakistan and returning with booming success.

Ten

The twist and turn of past policies

The Naga Peoples Convention (NPC) was a group made up of Naga people who were mostly pacifist and liberals. This group was the one that had been sturdily advocating: that Nagas have had enough of bloodshed and they must denounce the act of conflict and negotiate with the Government of India. Their opinion, on a general view, was not a total wrong assertion; it was explicable. The Nagas had gone through a galore of pain and sufferings in the course of fighting; but plunging into accord without the main stakeholder on board, which is 'the FGN,' was not a great idea. It would be like dressing an old sore and getting wounded again.

The matter of fact is, ever since 1957, NPC had been buzzing around the Indian Government's bid to offer them a statehood. NPC was left with a limited prospect of attaining a separate state from Assam. It is probable that India was proud of her varied cultural greatness, and was in no way inclined to gift away these Hills from her map. It seemed the only way to slake her thirst was to come under her charter. Nevertheless, for Nagas to come under the shade of the Indian constitution would be disrespectful to thousands of brave soldiers who had given up their life for the cause. The lure of a separate statehood endowed to Nagas was all bells and whistles. It was just a ploy to split the Nagas along territorial and tribal lines; a complete sell-out of innate rights on the end of NPC and a total tip-over to where Gen. Kaito and the Federal Government were heading. The latter was drenched thick and thin on the course of their struggle to free the Nagas, and it's clear they would straighten out with nothing less than a sovereign nation.

By March 1963, Gen. Kaito had returned successfully from the daring foreign trip with the first batch of his highly trained guerrillas, and brought with him a bulk of weapon supplies from East Pakistan to keep the freedom movement aflame in the Naga Hills. He was, however, dismayed when he returned home and observed the political tragedy that had taken shape during his absence. By that time, the Naga Peoples Convention had already negotiated for a separate State and the arrangements were already on the threshold.

The bill was passed in the Indian Parliament and an interim body was created in the Naga Hills on February 18, 1963, with Dr. Imkongliba Ao as its chairman. The interim body was dissolved nine months later by the Governor of Assam, and on December 1, 1963, a new state known as Nagaland was officially inaugurated by Dr. S. Radhakrishnan, the then President of India. Nagaland was declared as the 16th State under the Indian Union. A month later, on January 24, 1964, the first state Assembly election was launched and P. Shilu Ao was elected the first Chief Minister of Nagaland.

NPC was indeed the largest apparatus used by the Indian Government to diffuse the freedom fervour in the minds of the Naga people. It is evident that the first form of collapse of the Naga political issue was the signing of the 16th point of agreement by the Naga Peoples Convention. In fact, NPC did urge the FGN to dialogue and secede out of Assam State, but FGN was unmoved on the matter; they declined. Had NPC parleyed with the Government of India with the mandate of Federal Government of Nagaland, the Accord would have been a success. But there is not the slightest doubt, FGN with regards to the manifestation of the Naga statehood, was entirely out of perspective.

Even as the standoff continued between the pro-Indian Nagas and Federal Naga leaders over the statehood issue, on January 3, 1963, when General Kaito was still on his journey homeward FGN brought about a restructuring within the Federal set-up. General Kaito Sukhai was set to be allotted the Keya Kilonser (Defence minister) in the new FGN ministry, and had to resign the position of Commander-in-chief. General Kaito was quite reluctant to pass the Commander-in-chief position to someone else, particularly at a crucial phase. While as much as he felt the inevitability to hold the post at that relevant juncture, he also felt he was given a raw deal.

Ever since the meeting with Phizo in London, the confidence General Kaito pooled on the political wing had receded, which was why he had some other big plan as well, which he had not openly revealed. Also, he was plainly aware that hard times were on the cards, and the inkling he had at that point was that none could pedal the post of army chief as he could; fair enough, it was seemingly true. When General Kaito and Maj. Gen. Mowu visited London in late 1962; the political position of Phizo in London was utterly disappointing in contrast to what they had expected; as a result, Kaito picked a bone with his leader and came home fuming with an array of shocking details. In a concise statement, he stated to the FGN leaders, as quoted in Scato Swu's 'Hails and blames.'

"It would be folly of the Nagas to bank upon the President of NNC in regards to the strategy of approach towards Naga sovereignty in the external context."

He added, "Nagas must have an Army Government to attract more eyes of the outside world, or else we shall perish by Indian atrocities."

Maj. Gen. Mowu who was none other than the nephew of Phizo also remarked. "Things prevailing on Naga Londoner are not clear and quite unfavourable and improvements are not likely to come."

After Kaito's return from London to Naga Hills, he asked three questions to Scato Swu, the President of FGN; "Who were the people that selected Phizo to be our spokesman?"

To which Scato answered, "I was neither present during the selection of the spokesman nor did I know the names of the people that made the selection."

Again Kaito asked Scato, "Do you have faith in him?"

Scato replied, "Yes I do. If there is anything wrong, we will take it to the people, when the fullness of time comes."

Lastly, Kaito questioned, "Do you think Nagas can continue to perish without the knowledge of the outside world?"

Scato replied, "That is impossible; the NNC President ought to tell the Nagas frankly of his inability, in case he is facing a situation. But this, he has not revealed to us so far. So let us be patient, we will give him some more time and see what happens, and let the people decide." In fact, Kughato, having a perceptive mind, had said that some changes in the plan would be brought to the Federal Government when his brother Kaito and Maj. Gen. Mowu returned from the London and Pakistan trip, and it happened.

Naga unity was in danger, and the anti-elements scheming with Indian authorities were at loggerheads with the Federal workforce. To make things worse, Federal leaders within were at the crucial juncture of saving the accord from the malady of tribalism, which at the time was swelling to an immense scale. It was literal and becoming of Kaito why he felt that, at this stage, unity within the Nagas seems far greater than forfeiting his acclaimed job. Like all of the dedicated freedom fighters, Maj. Gen. Mowu Gwizantsu was no exception when it came to dedication, audacity, etc., but the fact is, even if Kaito was to be relieved of the Commander-in-chief post, the five top-ranking Generals in the seniority list who would be the probable successor, were Lt. Gen. Dusoi, Lt Gen. Makhen, Lt Gen. Zuheto Swu, Maj. Gen. Yeveto Zhimomi and Maj. Gen. Hokiye Swu. However, a situation arose where the FGN authorities had to decide between Naga Army service rules and Naga National unity. According to the Naga Army service rule, outstanding feats, efficiency and seniority would be the normal priorities for promotion or appointment to any ranks, which eventually was disregarded.

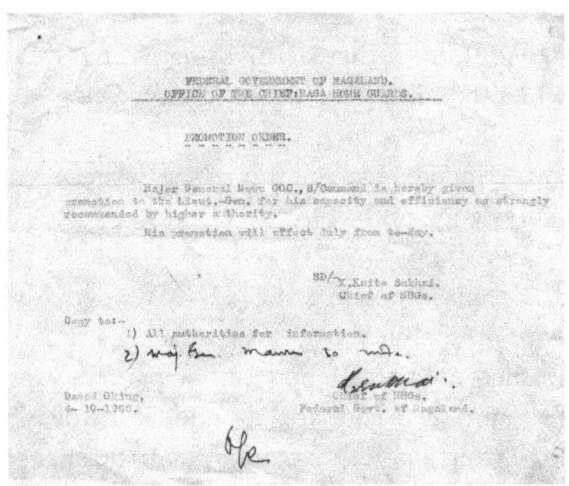

Promotion Order of Major General Mowu Gwizantsu to Lieutenant General issued by General Kaito Sukhai

Since the Naga fighters were the vital force behind the Federal Government and the basis for the Naga struggle, Kaito felt strongly that his forces mustn't be tampered with and neither should the position of armed force chief be taken lightly. He felt that anyone who desired to lead the Naga army should earn that position through their deeds and actions. For the position of army chief to be used as a lure to contain the grumblings of a particular group of people or individual would be a huge parody. Nevertheless, in contrast to the positive approach meant to be taken, the element of trust deficit radiating from some NNC leaders had unleashed tribalism. Thus, internal-bickering between the two powerful tribes, the Angamis and the Sümis, was taking place. In the case of Gen. Kaito Sukhai, the Naga Army was everything to him. He would, by any means, shield it from disruption. If truth be told, he was the one who had diligently reared it out of non-existence, and he had every right to pitch his opinion. On the other hand, General Kaito thought this was the moment for a litmus test and interlude, to renew the trust within the beaten tribesmen. So whether he liked it or not, he must contain the situation, which was why he yielded and eventually had to relent the position of Chief of Army to accept the post of Defence minister. Meanwhile, Major General Mowu was promoted to the Chief of Army on October 15, 1963.

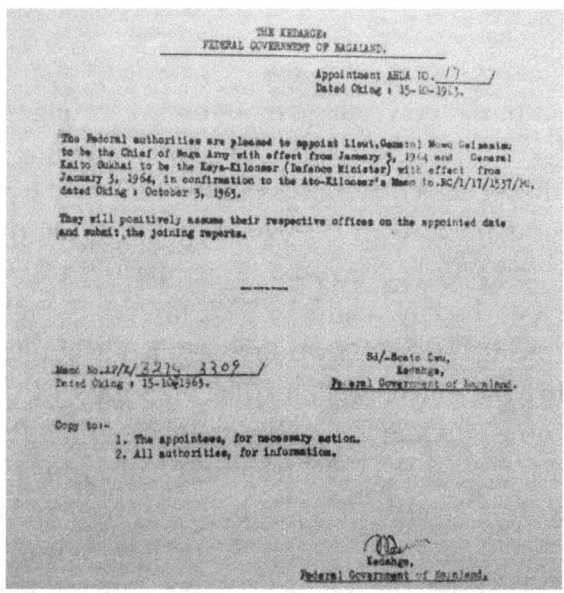

Dated 15th October 1963. The official promotion order of Lieutenant General Mowu to Chief of Naga Army and General Kaito to the Keya Kilonser (Defence Minister).

Despite differing opinions surfacing within the Federal structure, there was also a shower of optimism in 1964. A peace mission initiated by the Nagaland Baptist Church Council was convened on 24th February. A jolly tall peace crusader, Rev. Michael Scott of Great Britain, arrived in Nagaland. He learnt of the plight of the Naga people on his visit to India, following a stint with the Anti-Apartheid Movement in South Africa. That year in the spring, Rev. Michael Scott, along with some Nagaland Baptist Church Council members, arrived at Zupfu Naga army camp in Zelaingrong area to meet the FGN, Kedahge (President), Scato Swu. They held talks about the prospect of launching a truce between the Naga fighters and the Indian Government. Afterwards, some positivity subsisted from the meeting. A few months later, Rev. Michael Scott and his members even visited a Naga fighter's base camp at Khensa in the Ao area and Vishepu in the Sümi area. Vishepu camp was adjoining to the village of Hoshepu, the epicentre where the first Indo-Naga battle had erupted.

The invitation of the peace delegates into some strong revolutionary bastions was a distinct green light; this visit broke the ice between the two warring groups. Potential steps forward were hammered out during the visits. In view of that, on May 24, 1964, the first form of an official meeting between the representatives of FGN and the Nagaland Peace Mission members, took place at Sakrabama village in the Chakhesang area. FGN were represented by Zashei Hurie, the Angh of Japfu State, Biseto Medom, the Lota Kilonser (Agri Minister) and L. Zhenito Zhimomi, Tatar. The members of the Peace Mission comprised of B.P. Chalaiha, the incumbent Chief Minister of Assam, and the long-time veteran of Naga politics, Jaya Prakash Narayan, a staunch Gandhian, Rev. Michael Scott, Rev. Shiwoto Swunetho and some of the Nagaland Baptist Church Council members. The accord was signed and submitted to Nehru by B.P. Chaliha on May 26, 1964. However, it was unfortunate that Nehru did not have the chance to read it; he died in his sleep on May 27, 1964. Nevertheless, even after Lal Bahadur Shastri became the Prime Minister of India, he was concerned enough to look into the Naga issue. Five months and many efforts later, the hard work of the Nagaland Peace Mission members did pay off; both the Indian Government and the Federal Government of Nagaland, gave a positive nod to have a parley. On September 23, 1964, the first Indo-Naga ceasefire summit took place on a freshly designated Peace Camp Chedema. The theme of the Peace talk was: "Let us forgive to forget, let us agree to disagree." India was represented by Y.D. Gundevia, the Foreign Secretary, while Zashei Hurie, the Angh, Isak Swu Foreign Secretary and Brigadier Thinoselie Medom represented the FGN. The meeting kicked off in an upbeat note at Chedema peace summit, and conciliation between the Naga nationalists and New Delhi began in earnest. By early 1965, the peace mission practically came into effect within Nagaland.

While the Indian authority duly acknowledged Rev. Michael Scott's gamble on the peace mission, at the same time, they were also vigilant regarding his conduct. At this stage, he could not be too involved with Nagas, as his rights to interfere into the Naga issue was limited to an extent by the Indian Government. The deportation was likely to arrive anytime soon if the means of his approach on the Naga issue should irk New Delhi, and so his participation must be meticulous. The circumstances, which he also clearly stated to the FGN leaders on more than one occasion; "We truly sympathise with the cause of the Naga people, but at the same time, we also cannot be an enemy of India."

The Year 1965 began with many events and uncertainty. The device of the peace mission was in some way working to its tune between New Delhi and FGN. Still, the slew of false alarmists and the distrust sandwiched amidst the Naga tribesmen had started taking a toll on the peace talks. Unconfirmed reports were being circulated. At the same time, what could be a menacing report to New Delhi, was that their Intelligence radar had established news of Lt. Gen. Zuheto Swu's return from Alee command with about 1,000 highly trained Naga guerrillas, along with a range of war supplies from East Pakistan.

Zuheto's men had trekked from Chittagong, southeast Bangladesh into Chin Hills Burma.

From dusk to dawn, the access from Assam's old Chachar corridor was also patrolled by Indian troops. However, the Naga fighters were skilfully dodging through both routes, all the more baffling for the Indian securities, unsure whether to thwart off the Burmese rim or the Chachar passage. There was no fret for Zuheto and his men for they would be en route to Somra-tract via Chittagong, where their chief Kaito had already fortified his bastion. General Kaito's garrison in the 'No man's land' the later 'Somra Tract' situated between the western Burmese flank and northeastern India, was set up like a typical secured Indian camp. It was fenced with irons sheets and partly walled with concrete, and also, the issue of weapons didn't arise for General Kaito. In fact, likely to be fascinated, many questions did crop up to Indian authorities, why and who was providing the building materials and war supplies to this young General, and how did he haul in the building materials? Not so vague to Indians, there were some powerful external hands involved.

Press clipping: Indian Government trying to prevent the Naga guerrillas from entering the border.

The picture was clear; following the signing of the ceasefire agreement, the links with the revolutionaries had turned sour. The Naga armed wing was operating in contrast to the tactics of the political wing of the Federal Government of Nagaland. General Kaito was not satisfied with the peace talks. Peace talk to him was just playacting; an attempt by the Indian regime to dampen the spirit of freedom of the Naga people. He was running out of patience; sitting around all month and year-long with nothing more to do other than watch the prattling of political discourse with no fruitful result. Out of annoyance, he ridiculed the 'peace talk' as 'piss talk' and the Federal Government as the 'Funeral Government.' Further, even if he had to give the nod to the ceasefire accord, he insisted that the ceasefire must be endorsed by the United Nations, and should be incorporated under the effectual control of the United Nations, else the accord was doomed to be shallow. In the least, why can't the senior politicians even consult him on the matter? His armed force, as the backbone of the movement, should have been kept informed; but his influence was declining.

Oddball or unruly, whatever they called him, one thing the politician should be aware of, General Kaito wasn't a man to be easily deterred, especially when vital events were brewing. Moreover, he was the Defence Minister of the Federal set-up, and hence they should have consulted him on the affair, but that didn't come about. It was certain that sooner or later, some trouble would surface when the denial was coming from an individual who was much more committed to sacrificing whatever it takes, for the Movement. General Kaito let loose his fury! Despite his displeasure with the talks, he had given space and time to the peace mission for a period; but his patience had run out. The more he waited, the more the Movement declined. Further, the signs of the enemy getting the better of them was pretty noticeable. And how long could he endure the hush-hush behind his back, which was apparent? As expected, after some time, the young leader started to hone out his plan.

When Kaito expressed his strong displeasure to the political seniors, he was strongly backed by Mowu. He held classified talks with Mowu and some of his comrades about the political division over the matter. Mowu agreed with Kaito's view, as he felt that he too had been shunted out by the senior politicians, and it was not proper for the Political wing to have side-lined the two military leaders from the ceasefire talks.

Just as the peace talks were ensuing, General Kaito placed a proposal before the FGN leaders for charting out an Army Zone. The reason he wanted to establish an army zone within the ceasefire zone, was because the Government of India was plainly playing a dual diversion. On the one hand they had crossed their legs for talks, while on the other, they were full of activity, pooling their Jawans and establishing military control bases in Nagaland. The strategy of India was clear; it was to soothe down the freedom fervour under the guise of a ceasefire. He felt that if the Indian authorities were messing around with the Nagas, the Nagas must not give-in easily and be fooled. Furthermore, his fighters were also passing time with no distinct purpose. He furiously questioned the Federal Regime, "Who will be liable if the peace mission fails," the politicians couldn't give him a satisfactory response; none would dare to give an assurance; yet they were obstinate. In the meantime, encamped somewhere in the thick Burmese jungle, Lt. Gen. Zuheto had also warned his men against any defection under cover of a ceasefire.

General Mowu, now an army chief, supported Kaito's opinion. Mowu ranted out his tirade at the senior politicians on the conclave of Tatar Hoho. In the meantime, Kaito sent some of his men to blow up the NE railway line passing through Assam and Nagaland with the intention of expressing his displeasure over the ongoing talks and to send a signal that the Naga Army should not be taken lightly. Interestingly, the dynamite did not go off. Kaito was waiting impatiently for his men to return. Mowu was also waiting for the news. Later, Kaito came back laughing, and blurted out. "Oh Mowu, I sent the wrong men to blow up the track. They didn't know the positive and negative fuses." Both armed leaders had a hearty laugh over the episode. Shortly, when the news spread about Kaito's nerves to blow up the track, the politicians were pretty troubled. Thereafter, the rapport between the fighters and the political division were not too sound. The political wing left Zashei Huire, and his team to keep jabbering and thumping their fists on the peace table while, deep inside the jungles, Kaito and Mowu were busy stirring up the fighting ranks. And following Kaito's dynamite scare, most of the communications sent to the headquarters throughout the talks were henceforth condensed before it was endorsed by the armed wing.

In the intervening time, Rev. Michael Scott was going steadfast to the cause. He was busy troubleshooting between the FGN and the Indian Government, but possibly, on some occasions, he may have breached the line drawn by the Indian Government. Perhaps he was too outspoken about the Naga issue and had the intention of internationalising it. That was what New Delhi thought of him, and indeed, soon enough he was deported from India. It can be ascribed that Scott played the first-ever, and the key role, in driving the 'peace mission' into the Hills. His efforts opened a window of cessation to what was then running into more than a decade-and-a-half bloody conflict between two warring groups.

Many things transpired that year in 1966. India formally ended the war with Pakistan on January 10, on the Tashkent Agreement. The following day on January 11, Indian Prime Minister Lal Bahadur Shastri died, still in Tashkent, after what was reported to be a cardiac arrest. Right after Shastri's death, Indira Gandhi took over the role of Prime Minister. Back in the Naga Hills, the ceasefire was still holding, and the talks had been going on for nearly two years without much progress. It was not until winter 1966, when both sides acceded to a positive approval for ironing out the disparity; maybe it was time they needed to give a serious reflection on the talks. Naga envoys were willing to continue the dialogue without any hesitation. However, not the same old way of conveying messages through marionette diplomats, which to them was nothing more than a dull errand. Therefore, they felt that rather than being trapped in limbo, the leader of both parties must come to a table and commune in a practical approach.

Inch by inch, New Delhi and Naga revolutionary representatives both compromised towards a point where the only apparent remedy was to bring the leaders around the table. As progressive as it seemed, unless the higher-level talks took priority, it was still pointless. In a little while, the communication was relayed to the Indian Prime Minister that Nagas are keen to have a top plain discourse, which meant meeting with the Prime Minister herself. After all, the tables had turned. When informed on the affair, Indira Gandhi was equally pleased. How could she shy away from the path of Ahimsa? Hers was the Congress party, the political organisation which was more or less built upon the Gandhian principles. If Mahatma Gandhi was alive then, perhaps Nagas may not have been deprived of their aspirations for self-determination. As far as the Naga political issue was concerned, Indira Gandhi was not as conceited as her father Nehru, who had left a legacy that will forever stain the hearts of the Naga people. Unlike her father, Indira was rather disposed to make some suggestions on it. Yet, to the question of sovereignty, will she succumb to it? It was not likely. But, without further ado, on 18th February 1966, Indira Gandhi invited the Naga delegation to New Delhi and started penning down the list she could offer, so as to cease the political conflict at the earliest opportunity.

The young General Kaito wanted the armed wing to have their say in the political decisions, and also desired to make their presence felt in the negotiations with India. However, it felt like he was being blurred out of the image. It was clear to all and sundry that the presence of

General Kaito was the key reason why India was keen on moving towards political dialogue. India's first curiosity and prime concern was whether Kaito would support the peace talks or not. While it had arrived at a position wherein General Kaito was clearly not in favour of the talks, well, he was totally not against their continuation. But he was of the firm opinion that Nagas should negotiate hard for "Full independence." If not, the talks would be deemed worthless. In fact, Kaito had an alternative to dealing with every let-down; perhaps, even if the talks failed, he had a tact to keep the balls rolling. He would either be heading off to allied countries for aid, or he would install an Army government; whichever bound to be first. His brother, Kughato Sukhai, the Ato Kilonser of the FGN, would be leading no-nonsense talks with Indira Gandhi. Kaito sternly warned his brother, "I will gun you down myself if you sign the talks for anything less than sovereignty."

Isak Chishi Swu, then a modest bright young graduate, was serving as foreign Secretary of FGN. His father, Kuishe Swu, was among the first generation of Naga Christians, and had it not been for the persistence of the trio, Kaito, Kughato and Scato on Isak, he might have well ventured into his different calling. But as fate would have it, someday this soft-spoken lad had to take the position as the chairman of India's largest and most powerful insurgent group known as the NSCN-IM. "National Socialist Council of Nagalim" which in fact was a dissident group that stemmed out of the NNC-FGN after the latter signed a pact with Indian Government in 1975. That late winter of 1966, Isak, along with a number of FGN delegates, accompanied their Ato Kilonser to New Delhi to parley with the captivating Iron Lady of India. Indira Gandhi, in all her elegance, astute, glory and power, was premeditated on the Naga issue. To a well-planned policy of the typical shrewd Indian wits, the other members of the Federal delegation apart from the Ato Kilonser, were barred from the first phase of discussion, lest they hinder the talks. The other members were vigilant and brooded over the chance that at this stage. Their

Ato Kilonser, however, upright as he might be, if left alone, would perhaps yield to the trickery of the Indian Prime Minister. And so they did not approve Kughato meeting her in private, albeit he was the person in command of the Federal Government. This was not normally how Naga people went about doing things; most often their leaders are trusted with their all. But in fact, these were times when suspicions were tiptoeing over the slight rustle of leaves, and therefore even a 'possibility' was too much to let out of sight. Regardless, the Indian Prime Minister held a one-to-one discourse with Kughato.

No details escaped unseen from the intense eyes of Kughato's delegation. Therefore, what came to light after the talks that commenced between Mrs. Gandhi and Mr. Kughato Sukhai, was no longer a secret; it was revealed that wily Indira did tried to persuade Kughato to accept a deal within the union. Kughato was offered the top position in a status which could be worked out later, but that offer wasn't on Ato Kilonser's agenda, he was adamant. Kughato being the best mind in the business, understood his trades well. He knew what was negotiable, and Indira's proposal did not seem too unreasonable to him. It was apparent that India should not ascend above or perhaps won't degrade the Nagas much down below that offer. Kughato could grasp the main motive of Indira in the first place; she wanted an exigency to bring an end to the killings as far as both parties were concerned. Thus, more autonomy was offered as a gamble. She proposed to offer what could be a better deal than her earlier bid; a status not accorded to any other state yet, nor would it ever be. Kughato was not keen, however. Indira overtly restated it, but still Kughato declined the offer.

At the end of the six-round talks, the ultimate word of Mrs. Indira Gandhi was, "Mr. Sukhai, you take it all but not Sovereignty," to which Kughato Sukhai candidly replied, "I won't take it all, other than Sovereignty," besides, Kughato also said, "Madam even if I agree to take your offer, I'm not a dictator. I am bound to consult my Tatar

Hoho (Member of Parliament). During the last segment of Kughato's dialogues with Indira Gandhi, Zimik Ramyo, one of the senior members among Kughato's delegation at the talks, expounded to the other Naga entourage, not to be swayed over by the Ato Kilonser's words; Biseto Medom and others also voiced that, "It's better to stay under the Indian Government, rather than being underneath the Sümi's leadership." It clearly showed that they carried the voices of hatred and mistaken belief. But if truth be told, these negative feelings had not stemmed out of themselves; it was the seeds sown by the opponents to segregate the age-old kinship between the brotherhoods, which was already achieved. Perhaps Ramyo and his patrons believed that Naga people would still be under the Sümi's dominion, even if India liberated them; and they don't fancy that. A totally wrong notion coming from seasoned leaders which was really unfortunate. Thus, Indira Gandhi told the Ato Kilonser, "Kughato, it is ill-fated that your house is on fire, and you have to extinguish it." That was the end of the discussion. Without any contract or commitment, the talks ended in stalemate. Of course, Kughato had kept the Naga political rights intact for future generations which still holds today, while the great irony was that those leaders who were feeling uneasy over the speculation that Sümis under Kughato, might yield to the Indian offer, were severely at odds by means of Kughato's discourse with the Indian Prime Minster. They were the ones who gave life to the most infamous political blunder in Asia known as 'The Shillong Accord,' in 1975.

Ato Kilonser Kughato Sukhai (extreme left) with his delegates at Six Round Talks New-Delhi meeting with Indian Prime Minister Indira Gandhi (facing the delegation).

Reports on Naga talks

Unrest and violence on the North-Eastern part of the sub-continent at that juncture had left India's reputation badly stained in the eyes of the world. The birth place of non-violence was visibly tainted, and thereafter would continue in a long run. About the talks, whether Kughato thrived or not wasn't much of a topic to be mused over; it was rather the splits within the Nagas which was severe. A factor of distrust had developed between revered friendships and cherished brotherhood. Fears and suspicions lurking within the revolutionary channels had soared. After Kughato's return to the Hills, he was harshly criticised. Many outrageous charges were levelled against him. It was alleged that he had accepted the bribe from the Indian authority to trade away Naga sovereignty - an absolute lie. It was adversarial elements scoring points within the Naga political leadership. There was also a rumour doing the rounds among the locals, that Kughato was having an affair with Indira Gandhi; amusing indeed. A stream of distrust and hatred devised by the adversary had seeped through the tiny fracture opened up by some disgruntled Naga leaders.

It is indeed a bitter pill to swallow, but apparently the Sümi leadership had left the ranks green-eyed, and it was not strange because envy is one of the common human frailties. And yes, it is a well-known fact, that during that period, Sümis' had betrothed almost the entire top trappings of the FGN. Kaito Sukhai, the finest among the best, was Chief of Federal armed wing. His brother Kughato Sukhai, the one who led the talks with Mrs. Gandhi, was the Prime Minister FGN. The powerful pair were further boosted by the presence of their brother-in-law, Scato Swu, who was none other than the President of FGN. To define it more explicitly, it was a strong-wielded trident inside the FGN set-up, which again was greatly buttressed by the admirable partaking of the other formidable Sümi leaders, like Angh I.K Zuheshe, Nixukhu Zhimomi, Lt. Gen. Zuheto Swu, Maj. Gen. Yeveto Zhimomi, Maj. Gen. Hokiye Chishi, Isak Chishi Swu, Kuhovi Zhimomi, Zukiye Zhimomi and scores of other gallant partners of Kaito. It must also be acknowledged that none of these leaders lacked the due democratic norms while earning their position. Each of these individuals had delivered their superlative sacrifices in times of National emergency, to earn their place in the Naga Federal hierarchy.

Late Scato Swu the second Kedahge (President) Federal Government of Nagaland and brother-in-law of Kaito and Kughato.

The position of the Sümi tribesmen was elevated more to grandeur by Kaito's remarkable exploits in the Hills. His role was unequalled in Naga quest for freedom. He was loved, feared, hated and prized; reviled and admired by many of the Indian military commanders. They openly praised him for his daring feats. Every so often, the young General chuckled and flattered himself, saying, "These days, Indian commanders have emulated my guerrilla war techniques." To those who knew him in the flesh, he may not be a superhero; nonetheless, he stood out as a true symbol of hope. His feats were a flicker of hope to the exploited.

What many did not realise was, it was not a painless task to be a leader of Naga Freedom Movement in those days. In fact, from 1955 to 1990, Nagas had lost thousands of precious lives in the course of her struggle for Self-determination, and in the end, half of them were

Sümis. It was in the bloodiest and most agonizing era in the history of the Naga people, wherein the leadership gave their best, in a colossal attempt to steer the fraught Nagas into citizens of a free nation. In the course of achieving Naga Sovereignty, each and all of their possessions were sacrificed upon the National altar. This included influencing almost their entire Sümi youths to give up their education to serve in the Freedom Movement. Their families endured an excruciating agony. It felt as if they had tasted the entire cup of suffering. But lauding their effort seemed too much for most; they were instead despised, vilified and deemed as traitors. Such phenomenon was the main basis that sadly swamped the Naga political affairs during the late 1960s and early 70s.

In the mainstream leadership, the first Chief Minister of Nagaland, P. Shilu Ao, was ousted, and in his place was elected the courteous TN. Angami. Yet for now, it wasn't the mainstream politics that mattered; it was the grim development within the de facto federal fold that got people totally immersed with curiosity and fear. Opinions between the revolutionaries on the subject of Indo-Naga talks, had revolved on bad terms, and worse, baffled by Kaito's outburst over Beijing link. The Federal politicians had a series of meetings in the Rengma Naga area where the leaders tried to calm the fuming General. The young leader was seething with rage over the decision of Federal Headquarter to leave him out of this venture, albeit he was the brainchild behind this go-east-policy. Conditions were ideal when he put forth a bid to politicians to link up with Beijing, so as to externalise the Naga issue. Then, the matter was undecided; Kaito's plan to bond with the dragons was purely based on a physical and material perspective, and had nothing to do with communistic ideology. But most were wavering over the issue that Naga, being projected as a Christian nation, shouldn't have bond with communism. It was not appropriate. Kaito, however, proclaimed, "Let alone asking help from China, I would even take the help of the devil to achieve Naga Sovereignty," However bad this line may sound, it proves how determined Kaito was. Leaving aside the argument and given the inevitability of the situation, Kaito had in advance, prepared 200 of his best men to trek into China; the plan was simple yet original. It seemed UNO had reduced the Naga issue to something trifling; hence, only if he could tie up with a larger nation like China - as ridiculous it may seem to others - it would definitely ring bells at the United Nations and, of course, bonding with China would certainly have an impact on the external ranks. With these designs in mind, Kaito initiated his plan to have a strong link with China. He appealed to the FGN President to fund him some money to prepare for this mission, but the latter turned down his demands. Later on it came to the attention of General Kaito how the Federal politicians had started making use of his policy without him being aware of it. Nagas, comprising of more than 100 fighters under the command of Brigadier. Thinoselie Keyho and Thuingaleng Muivah, had left for China. Again, by December 8 1967, the second batch consisting of 312 fighters led by Gen. Mowu Gwizantsu and Isak Chishi Swu as special emissary of the FGN, were bound for China. It ought to be seen as a mistake on the part of the politicians, that Kaito excluded from such a crucial operation. Wasn't Kaito the fittest of all? Indisputably, he was second to none when such a perilous and vital mission was on the cards; above and beyond, he was the first to put forward the plan and was very eager to go out. Afterwards, it was said that China too was left dismayed on the non-arrival of General Kaito; the news of this young General's bravery and brilliant war strategies had also spread to the Chinese officials. They had been anticipating meeting him but were disappointed when they learnt about his non-arrival.

Maybe there were some explanations from the senior politicians as to why Kaito could not be sent on the Chinese mission. But even so, the grounds for leaving him out of this vital mission did not seem substantial enough to placate this young leader. Who shaped the Naga Army? It was Kaito. Who led the first batches of fighters into the Pakistani base? It was him. Who launched major battles with

Indian forces and busted off the Burmese Army on the other side many a time; it was him all along. Whatever his significance was to the movement; lately, Kaito was being considered as the dark horse in the midst of the entire Federal leaders. Rapidly, in a row, all of his dealings and proposals were deemed as if he was asking for the moon.

Five years earlier, when the Sino-Indian war was at its peak, Kaito had faultlessly devised a plan to back up the People's Republic of China, so that the latter could in turn help them recognise and declare the Naga Hills as an independent nation. But the formulation, whether China would have agreed or not, couldn't materialise, as during that period General Kaito was still staying in London, after leaving his fighters at the East-Pakistan military base for training. The truth is, as early as 1960, Kaito was in view and had been assessing that an army government in the case of the Naga issue would be more applicable. It was in 1962, while Kaito was in London, he had figured out the pitiable links that Nagas had in the Western Nation, so he prodded Phizo to have the East connection if the West wasn't of much help. Moreover, East would be far more easily accessible than the West, but his advice was regarded with scepticism from his senior. Even before the talks with the Indian Prime Minister had concluded, Kaito was certain that they were heading towards deadlock, and Nagaland after the deadlock would certainly be overwhelmed under the Indian military might. He could understand that it would be too late then; and that was why he told Mowu to make an alternative plan to confront the looming adversity. Kaito and Mowu shared a plan to set up an army government in the Naga Hills. "The plan will also attract more support from outside," Kaito enlightened. Mowu stood with him from the very start; but in the end, he too, was galvanised by the political wings and vacillated. And although Kaito's proposal did not appeal much to others back at home, he was not much dissuaded as it was obvious the majority of his guerrillas would stand by him.

At times when the policy of the politicians went off-beam, and while other observed in silence, it was typical of Kaito to overtly display a racket with no dread of elders. By and large, Kaito wasn't happy with the suppressive nature of the political wing over the armed wing. The politicians consisted mainly of seniors and the educated, whereas the armed wing comprised of naïve younger blood whose voices tended to be drowned out by the weight of the seniors in the Federal structure almost all the time. In their hearts, the fighters agreed with Kaito's concept that it was the formidable fighters that the Indian leaders were keen on negotiating with, not Federal politicians. But the fact was, they could not match the clout of the political wing and instead decided to remain quiet. Unlike Kaito, Mowu and others in the non-Sümi areas, were quite restrained on some pertinent issues; Mowu would defy the elders every so often, but had gone quiet on these vital issues, which made General Kaito and his fighters suspicious.

In the face of all the adverse relationships within the tribesmen and the subsequent impasse of Indo-Naga talks, Kaito told the Nagas, "The review of these last few years has seen a growing tendency towards a great disintegration, which hindered the Nagas' way towards national unity and its goal. Nagas must learn from the experience and lessons from Vietnam, the examples of self-defeating with all its pride, courage and patriotism, and therefore we must consider giving a practical shape without in anyway weakening the defence of the Naga nation."

Gradually, the demand to declare an army government was felt to be essential to General Kaito and General Mowu. In contrast to his plan, and as expected, his proposal seemed extreme to the Federal politicians. It had stirred the hornet's nest. It was said that Kaito's elder brother Kughato, should have restrained the young general. In fact, Kughato Sukhai and his brother-in-law Scato Swu, were both above reproach, particularly on this matter, for they had strongly opposed

Kaito's bid to form an army government. They were of the view that military government would put more importance on the barrel of a gun, rather than public interest. Military dictators normally do more harm to public sentiment than win their confidence, Democracy and civil rights would be directly or indirectly suppressed. No public leaders would join the army government. However, it seemed no one could ever persuade or alter Kaito's decision to form an army government in Nagaland.

In the meantime, some people started creating a false propaganda that the young general was trying to sell off the Naga sovereign rights, when Kaito created his plan to form an army government and it made things tougher for him. Ironically, it later turned out that those people who had propagated against Kaito's formation of army government were the ones who traded away the Naga sovereign rights in the outline of the Shillong Accord. The question still stands today as to why they propagated that Kaito was going to trade away the Nagas rights, when they knew well that 'Kaito would fight to the death for Naga independence.' General Kaito then had a hard time convincing the other Naga leaders.

It was evident that forming an army government can bring influence and attract the interest of certain nations too. General Kaito and General Mowu experienced this when they were coming back from their first alee (foreign) command back in late 1962. But Kaito had also weighed up all aspects of the Naga political landscape, and then made up his own mind regarding the formation of the army government. According to him, the first thing was to gain more external support. It was clear to Kaito, that even if some countries were willing to assist, it's likely they would encounter politicians squabbling among themselves - "An argument with no possible end" was what Kaito defined, by contrast to his army government which would be more straight forward and pragmatic. The Indian authorities might well have perceived that a barking dog seldom bites, which aptly fitted the

Naga politicians state at that time. "The talk was all doldrums," Kaito reiterated; besides, he also stated that it was too expensive to have a typical government, especially in the climate of Indian Military aggression. The politicians had failed miserably to bring about any practical result on the Naga political affair. Even the top-level talks with the Indian Prime Minister had failed. According to Kaito, militarism was the only option left to unify the Naga brotherhood that had been left in shambles by the politicians. Kughato and Scato delayed General Kaito's plan by restraining him for around six months or so before declaring the army government. But they could no longer hold him back.

Two months earlier, before the formation of the army government, an important meeting took place between General Kaito and General Mowu at Shepourmaramth, for the final preparation of an army government. It was evident that General Mowu and also the other powerful commanders had agreed to form an army government when the advantages of it were laid out. But it needed guts to trigger such a great plan. They slothfully waited for each other to take the first step. General Mowu and General Zuheto knew there could be a number of consequences. If they failed, the penalty was going to be severe, and none of them wanted to be the first one to stick their neck out. General Mowu sent Lt. Col J.P Vikugha to Kaito on three occasions, and apprised General Kaito to take the primary bait. Kaito had already detected the faltering among his commanders. Kaito was ever willing to flag off the plan, hence, he had a brief talk with Mowu. They decided to go with a bang simultaneously, and divide the regions evenly between them. Kaito would persuade and take charge of the Eastern and Central Naga regions, while Mowu would take control of the Southern, Northern and Western region and thereafter, they would pursue the plan together.

Disappointingly, all of a sudden, General Mowu went incognito at the last minute. He started acting unconcerned, and it was apparent that he had betrayed his Chief Kaito. Kaito went accordingly as planned and declared the army government at Litami village Zunheboto on June 17, 1967, and reached General Mowu's headquarters at Shepoumaramth, the next day, only to find General Mowu was missing. It was later learnt that at the time, Mowu was staying at Rano M. Shaiza's place at Kohima.

J.P Vikugha (now 82 years old) former Lt. Colonel and Signal Corps commander Naga Army was with General Kaito during the formation of Army Government.

Everything was happening too fast. To Kaito, it was about time that every single bullet had its worth. And ever since the talks, very few had been fired. The young General was now amassing ammunition for his new venture. This time he was draining out the treasuries and arm stocks from the same reserves he had filled earlier with the supplies he had hauled in from East Pakistan, as well as those captured from rival troops. However, his raids didn't involve all the Federal armouries, but he was pillaging those camps which, according to him, were dormant and were not likely to give an allegiance to the risk he was going to take. The loot from these raids would be transferred to an active segment which he deemed necessary so to implement his plan. The swiftness of the raid would be the priority. He hoped that none of his selected squad for this new venture would be required to pull a trigger against the division of Naga fighters that were opposed to his army government.

Summer was at its peak, and the day was burning hot in mid-June. Sentries manning the gates of the camp at western fringes of the Chakhesang area were feeling drowsy and moving about sluggishly. It was like any normal day - the weather, the routine, everything was as normal. And of course, some news was adrift about the bleak development that was taking place within the Federal leaders, which had reached the earshot of the camp inmates. However, nothing unforeseen seemed likely to happen at this peaceful site. The place was operating serenely, free from the bustle of the local populace, until a small band of armed fighters led by the young General, alighted from his Nissan jeep, and marched straight into the camp. General Kaito's men stepped in, and swiftly disarmed the guards and the other fighters inside. After a while they sealed off the entire site and made a clean sweep of the stuff they had come for. The booty included a fair number of weapons and half a dozen radios sets. While stuffing the spoils into the sack, some of them found a huge stash of currency; it was the money General Kaito had brought from Pakistan. Along with the war supplies, the money was also loaded into the jeep and carried away to Sümi Naga country. Interestingly, some of Kaito's tribesmen, who had come as guests to this camp the previous night, also left with this young leader. It appeared that Naga fighters, particularly the Sümis, could not envisage the survival of the movement without Kaito in the picture.

One of the plundered garrisons belonged to none other than his military successor and the then Federal armed Chief, General Mowu. Luckily or unluckily, Mowu was not at the camp that day. "It is a coup, but will be a bloodless takeover if you stick with me," Kaito informed the inmates of the despoiled camp, who consisted mostly of Angamis and Chakhesangs. The young General's broad daylight raid of the camp, which literally falls under the chief of army, was bizarrely audacious. However, those senior leaders who knew Kaito well, were not surprised with his typical guts. Mowu, who was his strongest ally at one point in time, was now in the opposing camp, and he had no choice but to weaken him. Any loophole left behind the scene would indicate a weakness in his plan; he ought to contain them all; perhaps that's the nature of this gamble.

Before coming back to his hometown, Zunheboto, he had a brief meeting with the elders of Chakhesang tribe. Among his band, was a younger brother of General Dusoi Chakhesang, who was now an aide to the young leader. Kaito explained to the elders why, in his view, the present FGN politicians were beating around the bush. He also shared some reasons why and how his army government could bring a new hope to the Nagas. He had devised his plan well, and now was taking it to another level.

Meanwhile, at Chedema peace camp, a huge commotion had erupted over the reports of armoury raids by General Kaito. Senior Federal leaders stationed there were in utter panic, several of them were openly critical of Ato Kilonser Kughato Sukhai, who became a scapegoat for not restraining his brother. Ato Kilonser had tried to warn his brother on more than one occasion, but could not persuade him. Clearly, the seniors expected some blows from the heated young General, but not as hard as this; it was too sudden. To the Federal seniors, it seemed the Indian government had been able to infiltrate the movement through none other than their greatest military General, and that Kaito was operating at their behest. But the truth is, Kaito was acting on his own, he was never a man to be easily influenced by an enemy or anyone else. Furthermore, given the intensity of love, belief and sacrifices he had rendered to this movement, no costly price could buy him off, or persuade him to act against his own brethren. He was, rather, onto an ingenious plan of his own, and according to him this plan was the only means to revive the movement which otherwise was failing.

The young General and his fighters never took a break; they carried out raid after raid on the Federal camps in the Sümi and the Ao Naga areas, persuading most of them. Several divisions moved over to his side. The troops that moved to join him consisted mostly of Lothas and eastern Mao tribes. Among his followers were also the Aos, Rengmas, Changs, Yimchungers, Sangtams, Pochurys and more. Thousands of guerrillas owed allegiance to him. But one thing General Kaito did not have was the support of heavy-weight politicians. This was his one weakness, which could jeopardise his plan, since none of the elders had joined him yet on this quest. The greater hindrance was the breaking away of his influential commander, General Mowu Gwizantsu, who had gone off course from the actual arrangement, and furthermore, even Kaito's trusted partner, General Zuheto Swu, was not committed to the plan. The support of the larger tribes like the formidable Angamis, Chakesangs and Tangkhuls' were less, and it upset him.

Although there was division among the Nagas, the ceasefire with India was still in effect, and so the Naga revolutionaries could mix with ordinary Indians. During such times, those Indian Army Commanders, who in fact had admiration for this young Naga General, would often request him to come to their camps for dinner. On one occasion, General Manekshaw, the then GOC of Eastern Command Indian Army, came down to Kohima and instructed a Colonel to call up General Kaito's home line at Chandmari, Kohima, and invite him to the ancillary army camp located at Heritage bungalow, Kohima. The Colonel was told not to disclose to Kaito, that General Manekshaw would be in attendance, The Colonel made the call and dinner was proposed for 6 pm. Kaito agreed to their invitation. Huskha Yepthomi, the Personal Security Officer to General Kaito, keenly accompanied his chief to the Indian Army camp in Kohima town. To the surprise of both General Kaito and his PSO, the considerably tall and sturdy Indian General came inside the dining room where they were sitting with an Indian Colonel named Sethi. As soon as Manekshaw entered the room, he queried, which among the two Nagas is Kaito. The Indian Colonel pointed to the shorter gentleman. Kaito gleamed with ease and stepped forward to greet the Indian General. Observing Kaito from head to toe, Manekshaw momentarily paused with an obvious confused expression. He wasn't expecting the dreaded Naga General who had been wreaking havoc to the entire Indian ranks in the Northeast Indian region, would be this young charming lad. He was expecting someone older, maybe taller. General Manekshaw started the conversation by saying, "Would you mind if I address you as Mr Kaito." Kaito nodded calmly and said, "I won't mind." Manekshaw asked around twenty or so questions, some of which Kaito replied even without letting the Indian General complete his sentence. Seemingly, General Manekshaw was pretty impressed with the acumen of this Naga General, and a little later, started addressing him more politely as, "General Kaito" or "My dear General Kaito." They also had a hearty laugh at some of Kaito's crafty jokes. The conversation wound up by General Manekshaw advising Kaito, "Dear General Kaito, whatever happens, let us try to avoid an arms conflict between us."

General S.H.F.J. Manekshaw on his earlier years as Lieutenant General. He was one of only two Indian Generals who would later rise to the ranks of Field Marshal (Field Marshal is highest rank in the Indian Army which had been conferred to only two Indian Commander-in-Chiefs, one is General Manekshaw and the other General K.M. Cariappa).

Dr. Huskha Yepthomi, former President Sumi Hoho and former PSO (Personal Security Officer) of General Kaito Sukhai who accompanied General Kaito while meeting General Manekshaw

Little did the FGN politicians and the Indian authorities realise that while it gave the impression that Kaito was conniving with the enemy, in reality, he was getting the better of General Manekshaw and slowly bringing the Indian Government towards a position that would be advantageous to the Nagas. Everything had gone stealthily and perfectly as planned. Naturally, judging by the performance Kaito had enacted, the FGN politicians had the right to sense that their General was indeed heading in the wrong direction, because the game this astute young General was playing was not understandable by common minds. Sukhato Rotokha, who at the time was the Patkai State Council President and the senior member of the FGN, was also a distant cousin of Kaito. Two months prior to the hit on Kaito's life, Sukhato Rotokha recollected meeting him at Kohima. Despite having a difference in ideology over the formation of the army government, Kaito knew well that Sukhato Rotokha was a man of principle and could be trusted with secrets; so he told Sukhato Rotokha, *"Brother, my connection with the Indian Army is nothing more than a shady deal.*

You know, we've already had enough bloodshed, and now overriding them with our guns seems quite unlikely at this moment, while at the same time our politicians too have failed to go on with the talks. Therefore, I'm planning different tactics now; a strategy which would be very resourceful to our Movement. Later on, I will use this connection to strengthen my own Naga Army and salvage the presently declining, Naga National Movement. After that, we will fulfil our aspiration for our independent Nation." He further stated with seriousness on his face, "I could possibly be killed by my own Naga people in the course of this action. If I am killed before my plan is attained, then it will be a great loss for the Nagas, as Nagas will take a long time to achieve independence if I die. However, if I am to be killed after fulfilling my plan, I shall die content, because that means Nagas have achieved independence, and a dead man will have won a battle.

Dr. Sukhato Rotokha also known as Dr. H.S. Rotokha (now 87 years old) former Patkai State Council President and senior member of the FGN.

After Kaito's declaration of an army government, and the dismal rapport between the Federal structures, the bell began to chime with the alarming speculation that perhaps the worst episode for the Nagas was on the way. The last Indo-Naga talks concluded on October 7, 1967, with neither side giving-way to each other's terms. People were left apprehensive as the bitter animosities within the Federal set-up increased. In the face of all these medleys of speculation and happenings, Ato Kilonser Kughato Sukhai, felt the necessity to take a crucial step. A mutual gathering of the Federal leaders was urgently needed. The utmost priority was to sort out the division among the Naga leaders, so political talks could continue, since they were clearly on the verge of collapsing. Kughato wrote a single sentence letter to his Federal colleagues, "Either to renegotiate with India or to go to war with them, there's no alternative." A meeting was called for May 27, 1968, at peace camp Chedema, to discuss the given agenda.

That day, 33 FGN leaders, including five senior Naga Army officers, gathered. The meeting proceeded with everything going well, until to the utter surprise of Ato Klonser Kughato Sukhai and the other members; instead of discussing the set agenda, 'War, or to renegotiate with India,' some among them proposed that the 'Parliamentary' form of government, should be changed to 'Presidential' form of government. A strange pre-planned agenda came into place, and abrupt silence filled the meeting hall. The out-of-the-blue agenda had stunned most of them; they were at odds with it as it was not an original issue for which the meeting was called; it was rather a covert plan devised by some NNC members to technically remove Ato Kilonser Kughato Sukhai from his chair. Accordingly, on May 28, 1968, the Presidential Government was declared, with Mhiasiu Angami as president, and thereafter, all the top Sümi leaders and their staunch followers were stripped of their FGN ranks. Unfortunately, this unworthy tactic of the NNC, crippled the Nagas in the long run. The NNC divided the FGN for their self-interest, and the split sown then has lingered to this day. The brother-in-law duo, Kughato and Scato objective, was to build up a strong base and a smooth political tie between India and the Nagas, and after that they were going to invite the NNC President Phizo for a consensus settlement. But it was unfortunate that Phizo who was then taking political asylum in London, developed doubts and fears that the Sümi leaders were going to finish the game without him.

After the sixth round of talks came to deadlock, the remedy apparently was that the Naga leaders could come together and resolve the disparity within, and take a decisive step together; but that didn't come about.

Instead, the leaders disbanded among themselves. It was a phase of utter devastation for the Naga National Movement; what could be more distressing when the family itself was divided in times of peril and crucial moment, and what were the real options left after that?

Fear and doubt had once again overtaken the minds of the Naga people at large. They speculated as to whether their villages would be once again be set ablaze? Would people die of starvation? What added more qualms to their uneasiness, was the fact that the Indian government had learnt that hundreds of Naga fighters led by General Mowu, had darted off to China, and they speculated as to what might transpire after their return.

Whatever could be the price to thwart that India-bound, Chinese-trained squad, the Indian authorities were not going to waiver. By any means they were intent on preventing the return of Mowu's groups. Nagaland at that time was still under the spurious trance of an armistice pack, but an extensive number of Indian troops had clamped down every division of hills, and the entire strategic stretch of border was being restricted, day and night.

General Kaito had sensed that it was suicide for Mowu and his fighters to walk inside the Indian territory at that time, so he secretly formulated a brilliant plan to facilitate a safe channel for his comrade Mowu and others, before they stepped inside the enemy zone. Kaito planned to haul in a stock of essential supplies inside the Burmese corridor where the Indian troops had no right to enter. Thus, there he could feed his homecoming fighters, and let them stay secure and out of harm's way. The motive was to keep the Naga fighters at bay, far from the reach of the enemy, while at the same time he was preparing to bargain hard with the Indian government. But unfortunately General Kaito's assassination took place before that plan was put to purpose, and General Mowu's later arrival would instead take a wayward turn. Some people claimed that Kaito had deceived the Naga people, but looking closely, it is easily discernible that the amount of love and devotion he had for the Nagas and his nation was far greater than anything, and the Naga movement was everything to him. Therefore, even if some ill-feeling prevailed between him and the FGN politicians, he would never barter away the Naga rights for his personal interest. The formation of army government was rather an opportunity and a risk Kaito had taken to initiate his crafty plan. An intelligent man like him would not fall easily into the traps of the enemy.

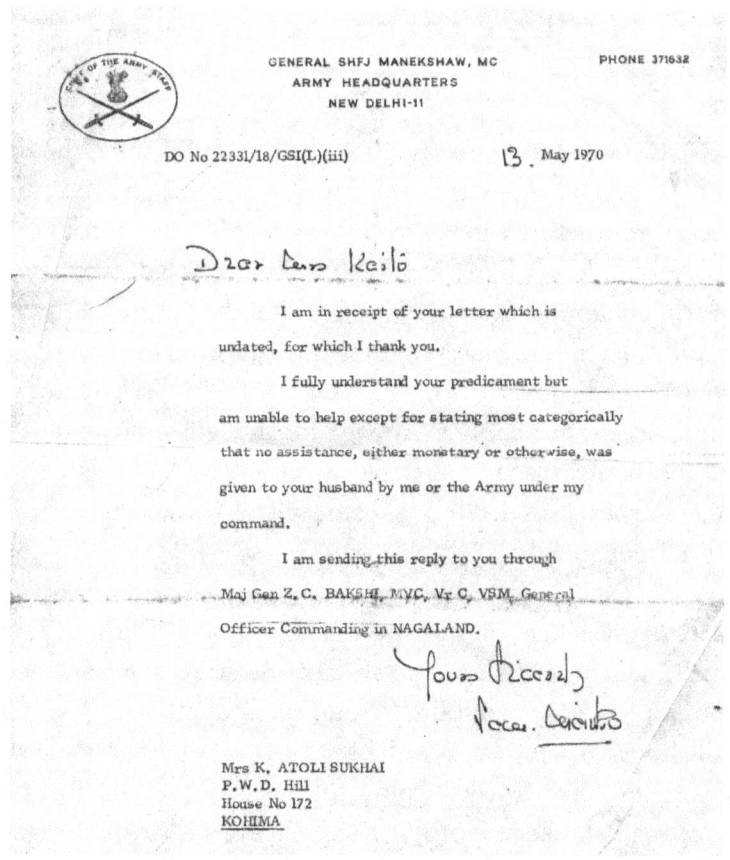

Indian Field Marshall General Manekshaw's letter to Kaito's wife after General Kaito's death which clears the negative perception some had about General Kaito. It states that General Kaito did not had any backing or assistance from the Indian Government during the formation of his Army Government

Eleven

The smothered star

"We live by deeds not by years"

August 3, 1968 was like any other regular day in Kohima; the sky was a lucid blue, a plain signal that the day would be bright and sunny. It was a usual routine in a lone street, shanty-town, Kohima. A line of small shops would open early at the first light, though they closed up much earlier before sundown. A good deal of the business functioning would follow later in the day. Then, the town would be swarming with customers, mostly government officials and their wives, clutching up the best delicacy they could rummage for the relish of their kitchens. On the footpaths, Naga womenfolk would spread out garden wares such as tomatoes, mustard leaves, yam, spring onion, beans, beehives, eggs, and other such local edible goods for sale.

It was late in the afternoon, the sun was already setting on the horizon. The sunshine had dried out the surface moisture from an incessant downpour a few days ago, but a strong smell of after-rain, sun baked soil, still lingered. An ant-like filament of pretty Naga damsels was down the alley, clad in their colourful gleaming shawls and pleated mekhelas, with baskets on their heads laden with fruits, vegetables and firewood, were heading gaily towards their village gate. Instead of groaning under the weight, the homebound damsels would cheer up the onlookers by humming in unison a melodic musing folk song, which seemed to resonate like a soothing 'recital in the breeze.' The walkway, which earlier had been teeming with Naga womenfolk selling their vegetables and goods, was already deserted. During the day, a football match was also played at Kohima local ground, and crowds were quite bustling, but now the crowd had visibly simmered down to a few slackers and homebound citizens.

For business communities, in particular, the non-locals, the fading of an orange beam on the western horizon was a natural reminder to close their shops and head home before darkness descended. One could not be so careless as to saunter around the town after the night crept in, as muggings or other threatening things often took place after dark. It was about 4:30 PM. A jeep was parked close to Kohima's lone all-purpose store named 'Dos and Co,' located near the present day, Razhu Point. Most of the onlookers didn't know that the two personalities who had parked their jeep there were none other than the famed Sümi Naga brother duo, Kaito and Kughato Sukhai. The more well-to-do Nagas would often crowd here to buy provisions or have a quick drink or two of the local brews before heading home.

Kughato was seated inside the jeep, while Kaito stepped out and strode towards the engine. He looked under the bonnet and was busily engrossed, checking the engine as the jeep was having some technical problem. At that time, there weren't many repair garages in the Hills, and the jeeps would frequently break down in the middle of the road. Locals had a hard time fixing them in those days, but with the passage of time, they gradually became more adept at repairing and putting them back on the road.

As the maxim goes, 'a loaded wagon makes no noises.' A secret arrangement had been established between a top authority and assassins; it was only a matter of time and place when the assassins would find their target. Neither Kaito, nor his elder brother Kughato, or their companions, had any preconceived notion that executing Kaito that day was planned. The assassins were already on the prowl, lurking nearby, watching the target's every move. Killing Kaito was a most significant assignment for them, so must the preparation had to be flawless. Certainly, at other times, Kaito was aware that he was being trailed by numerous Federal personnel to wherever he went, for reasons best known to them. But today, it was intended to be more than a trailing game. The plotters had passed an order to snub him out.

The time was 4:45 PM. A small number of shops were still open and a few amblers were clumsily walking down the street. At an intersection near an electric pole, 'Razhu point,' two young assassins draped in a Naga 'Lohe' shawl, between 15 to 20 yards away from the parked jeep, were intensely watching Kaito's every move. They were relieved to find that the General wasn't accompanied by any bodyguards or security personnel. They must have thought - today would be the perfect opportunity.

As Kaito crossed the road and walked towards the motor parts shop, perhaps to replace the defective parts of his jeep, the two assassins saw this as great timing to execute their job. Wrapped in a shawl, one assassin bolstered himself up, parted his shawl and held out his gun, already prepared to shoot. At that same instant, Kaito instinctively turned to face the assassin. His intuition may have warned him that something was amiss, that something bad was about to happen. Kaito, on impulse, covered up his abdomen with both his hands and turned towards the assassin; he recognized his face. The assassin parted his shawl and in a split second, fired bullets from the barrel of his gun from close range. Some penetrated Kaito's wrist and settled in his abdomen; the other bullets directly hit his abdomen. He had brushed off close-shave situations innumerable times, but fate had it, that day, he couldn't evade those bullets, and it was fatal. He fell to the ground with his hands still clutched to his belly. Kughato rushed towards his fallen brother, who by then was lying in a pool of blood.

The assassins ran to one of the narrow lanes piercing between two small shops and quickly disappeared into the maze of tracks and trails channelling through the old bamboo houses until out of sight. The bridle path which a person could cross at a time had been a winning ticket for assassins' getaway. Several people rushed to Kaito. It wasn't just the sound of gunfire that panicked them; it was the sight of Kaito, lying in a pool of blood that had them petrified. A sheer state of apprehension instantly filled the air.

Ranpal, a young Nepali who had a small shop next to the department store, was startled when he heard the sound of gunfire. He alighted from a long wooden bench set up just outside his shop. Along with other bystanders, he rushed towards the spot of the collapsed man. Ranpal and the other onlookers were evenly shocked as well as dismayed when they recognised the face of the injured man and realised it was none other than General Kaito Sukhai, a hero to many. Who had not heard of this daring and handsome General? His legend had spread not just across the Naga country or within the ranks of Indian military folds alone, but had stretched west as far as Great Britain, where he was dubbed 'The World's Youngest General,' the 'Born General,' and a 'Statesman,' by the BBC (British Broadcasting Corporation) and some leading British tabloids.

Vikuto, the General's younger brother, was some 200 yards away, driving another jeep, when Tolhopu, one of his brother's trusted companions, appeared out of the crowd and stopped him. A short time earlier, Vikuto had been sent by his brother Kaito to bring the jeep which was at home at Lower Chandmari. He was bringing the vehicle as instructed. Tolhopu informed him that his brother Kaito had been shot. Vikuto was badly shaken by the upsetting news, but he composed himself and rushed tensely towards the spot of his fallen brother and was the first person to pick him up. His eldest brother, Kughato, was still standing nearby, shell-shocked. Vikuto clearly remembers what his brother Kaito told him that day when he lifted him up on his lap, Kaito said, "Do not take me to the Naga Hospital, take me to Army hospital," He also said, "The assassin who shot me was one of my soldiers' who went to East Pakistan with me."

In those days, there were only two hospitals at Kohima; one was run by the Indian military, and the other by the state government, which was Naga hospital. At Kaito's behest, he was rushed to the Indian military hospital which was then located at P.R Hill, below the present-day Police Headquarters. He knew that if he was taken to the Naga hospital, the assassins' groups could come there to kill him. His safety was not guaranteed there, which was why his safest bet was the military hospital. The news about the incident had already spread. After some time, thousands of people began to crowd outside the military hospital, anxiously waiting to hear the fate of their famed leader. However, for security reasons, Kaito's youngest brother, Kuhoi, and his second younger brother, Vikuto, were the only civilians permitted inside the hospital to stay alongside their injured brother. Kuhoi, who was beside his injured brother's bed during the whole time, heard his brother Kaito saying, "I was shot because I loved the Nagas, and I have a feeling that I will die of this wound. If I die, my people should never take revenge on my assassins." Kaito knew that if he died, a tribal feud was imminent, and he did not fancy his death to be the source of enmity between people he loved most; even with his last breath, he would confront the rivalry between his people. Despite the blazing desire for revenge growing among the faithful followers of Kaito, eventually his last wish was honoured.

A horde of Indian army doctors went into an array of critical operations in an urgent bid to save Kaito's life. Then began the 18 hours long race against death. To those doctors trying to sustain his life, it was the shortest span of 18 hours. His relatives were planning to airlift him to Shillong, if his injury continued to threaten his life. Never was a man willing to fight for his life as much as Kaito. Repeatedly, he would say to the doctors, "How could this happen? These bullets cannot kill Kaito."

A few hours after his abdomen surgery, Kaito woke up groaning with pain; he was sedated with anaesthesia, but the pain was severe. Vikuto looked down at him, strained faced, and said, "You are going to be fine as doctors have operated on your wounds," but Kaito replied rather clumsily, "I can't even take a pee, so how could I survive?" Time was swiftly fading away and Kaito foresees certain death looming. He could endure the pain inflicted by the bullets on his flesh, but the pain wrecking inside his heart with the thought of the fate of his beloved Nagas and what they would be going through in the near future, was far more wrenching for him to bear. He said, *"I love Nagas, I sacrificed my life for the Nagas, but someone wanted to take away my life and I'm dying. My heart bleeds for the Nagas as I see more days of struggle in achieving the goal. Should I die, there will be splits, division and more killings amongst us."* Indeed, this saying was poured out from his heart. Kaito's assassins thought taking his life would bring an end to every hindrance, but they were proved wrong. After Kaito's death, and true to his words, the upsurge of divisions and killings among the Nagas spiralled like never before. During that crucial time of discord, a strong personality like Kaito was probably the only force that could have fused the Nagas together, which otherwise was drowning in a clutter of tribalism. Around 8 PM the same evening, his fever started to rise, and after a while he started muttering some faint words which were not intelligible to others. A few hours later, Kaito lost his consciousness. He had lost a massive quantity of blood; the white sheet under his bed was drenched red with blood even after the doctors had operated on him. The warrior's abdomen was badly damaged; the bullet had slashed his intestine similar to knife wound.

On the morning of August 4, precisely at 9 AM, an army doctor with an insignia of Lt. Colonel on his shoulder, though he was now draped in white surgical apparel, paced out with bated breath. He said that the General would have to be re-operated on as the bleeding on his wounds seemed to prevail even after the first stitch-up. The doctor also announced that they would be in dire need of blood for the second operation. As soon as the information passed out within the surrounding of the hospital, hundreds of Nagas, mostly youths, readily turned up to offer their blood. After a battery of tests, nine person's blood was transfused to Kaito, which included a unit of blood from his youngest brother, Kuhoi. The wound was too severe, and on top of that, it would be the second operation within an interval of ten hours or so. Only a miracle could save the dying General! Surgeons performed the task with less optimism. And in the end, a great attempt by the doctors to revive him failed. This time, the warrior couldn't survive the storm. Alas! Not even a hero could defy death; a few hours later at 11:30 AM General Kaito Sukhai succumbed to his injuries.

The same morning of his assassination at 7 AM, a 6-year-old girl was walking alone towards her Baptist English School which was sited some 200 yards away from the spot where General Kaito was shot. The young girl saw the spilled blood all over the pavement on which she was walking. She was petrified and tense when she saw the blood. Later on, she arrived at her school and told her friends about the spectacle she saw, and later at home she was informed by the elders that the blood was from a man named General Kaito. Little did she know that the sight of that blood would frequently stalk her mind to this day. She felt that meeting the family of General Kaito would somehow heal her from the encumbrance of that unpleasant scene. It was only recently that she met General Kaito's family. She said that she was indeed at peace now. That young girl was Dr. Hathling, who is currently the Chief Medical Officer of Peren District, Nagaland.

Very often, and even on that fateful day, his dear and near ones had warned him. "You ought to be more cautious with the adversaries around you." Then teasingly, he used to remark, "Do not worry. Only a golden bullet has my name written on it." Indeed, the golden bullet had him marked, albeit the 'golden bullet' was dispensed from the hands of the assassin who was brewed and nourished by some sorehead leaders, which regretfully found its end in none other than 'The greatest son of Naga soil that had ever lived.' Very lamentable indeed! The BBC and hordes of newspapers were sad to announce the death of 'The World's Youngest General.' It was such a tragic end to such an extraordinarily gifted leader, who parted his life early at the age of 35 years and 74 days, with yet a great deal of unfinished tasks.

It was a fanatical assassin who could not realise that he was killing the Nagas best chance for independence, or the greatest military genius of his era, and also the magnitude of impact that this young General could possibly have brought upon the fate of the Nagas had he been alive. Yet, he was shot in cold blood on that ill-fated evening. Had General Kaito survived that tragic shot, Naga history would have taken a different tide. The authenticity of the assassin's identity was alleged and conjectured on several people for more than half a century. But it was clearly revealed by Mr Visier Meyasetsu Sanyu in his autobiographical book 'The Naga Odyssey' (Page-135), which was released in 2017. "Captain Aruno, the brother of my sister-in-law Nizono, was ordered to carry out the *azah (order)*. This created personal turmoil as Aruno had admired and served under General Kaito before Kaito's defection from the Nationalist side. However, an order to implement an *azah* could not be denied. Aruno assassinated General Kaito on 3rd August 1968 in Kohima." Captain Aruno was an Angami Naga from Khonoma village; he was a loyal soldier to both General Mowu and General Kaito. Aruno was also among the first batch of Naga soldiers who went to East Pakistan with General Kaito in 1962.

Left to right, General Mowu and Captain Aruno

Kughato had warned Kaito that the time was not good for him to move out freely in Kohima; his brother-in-law Scato Swu too, on his part, had warned him more than once. That day his wife had also warned him not to go out, but it was Kaito's nature to casually disregard her and others by simply saying, "What have I done? My whole life I had gone through trials and ordeals for my people. I should have nothing to be troubled about; they, rather, should be proud of me." The path he picked for himself was never a burden for him, but in fact, his struggle was the hardest. There is no ravine, no flooded river, and no rugged trails of this hilly terrain that wasn't familiar with the drifting feet of Kaito. Well, at times, he might have had bad intuition of how he could be killed by anyone, maybe even his own people, but he was also assured that his people were well aware of the hard work he had delivered towards the cause and deep down in his heart, he strongly felt that no individual Naga would go to the extent of killing him. However, he was proven wrong in the end.

Kaito often went out encircled by five to six bodyguards, but on that fateful day, he went out alone to drop off his eldest brother Kughato, who was on his way to fetch his son from Meluri, Phek. Besides, the next day on 4th August, Kaito was planning to travel to his native Zunheboto, for reasons unknown to his followers; the motive for his journey he normally would announce at the last minute. Regretfully, that trip was never going to happen but would instead have to come about the other way round. When he was getting into the jeep for the last ride to town, his little son, Hoshepu, came running down from his play and saluted his father in a calm military approach. The General returned his salute for one last time!

Kaito often said, "Being a freedom fighter, life cannot promise you a natural death. You are prone to die either on the war front or possibly from the hands of enemy assassins. But to be killed by his own people whom he had given his best and loved the most was very unfortunate. Maybe by then, Kaito was aware of the bad times that were closing in on him. It was early 1968, and his eldest daughter Nagaholi was barely 8 years old. She was leaving for Kalimpong, West Bengal, for her schooling, while her father had come down to Dimapur rail station to see her off. She will always remember the moment when her father, who was tough as an old boot and not too often expressive, bade her adieu with runny eyes that day. Little did this young girl know that this would be the last goodbye from her father. Nagaholi was not informed of the news of her father's death until the fall of next winter when she returned home to her native, Zunheboto.

Before his mortal remains were carried off to his home, it was taken to Old Minister Hill, Kohima, at the residence of Supply Minister, Government of Nagaland, Ihezhe Zhimomi, for last respects. There at the Minister's residence, a glowing tribute was read out by several Naga leaders and people from different walks of life. His eldest brother Kughato Sukhai, and his elder sister Hotoli Swu, put up a brave face and pronounced a tear-jerking tribute. Kughato lamented, "Let alone the Sümis and his family, but Nagas have lost a great son and a true leader," for he knew Kaito at his best. The young general had married two wives, Khesheli, and Atoli, and had six children from them. For his children, there would be no cuddling or coat of arms from their daddy. This was the day when the six children, including the one in the mother's womb, were rendered fatherless. Despite everything that had befallen, Kughato gracefully declared that he would not avenge his brother's death, because it was the wish of his late brother that his assassin should be forgiven. It was not an easy call to make, but it was magnanimous of Kaito's family to consider that they shall not add salt to the injury; a further division to the already divided Nagas was inevitable if vengeance was to take its course.

The authors with Ihezhe Zhimomi (middle). Ihezhe was a former Government Minister of Nagaland. General Kaito's mortal remains were taken to his place for a brief farewell service at Kohima, before being flown to his Native place Zunheboto.

The whirling of the helicopter blades in the southwest of Kohima town, became increasingly audible as thousands of heavy-hearted Nagas, walking behind the motorcade laden with the mortal remains of the young leader, approached the helipad. In those days, apart from a, few government officers, Nagas rarely owned cars, and that was probably the largest cavalcade that Nagas had ever witnessed over the entire Hills. A fleet of more than 80 vehicles stirred down like a dawdling hill bound train and carried Kaito's mortal remains to Assam Rifles helipad ground, Kohima. The helicopter, accompanied by an Indian Army Commanding Officer, transported the mortal remains to Kaito's native place, Zunheboto. A wreath with glowing sentence inscribed, "To my new found friend," was also sent by his Indian counterpart, Field Marshal Sam Hormusji Framji Jamshedji Manekshaw, popularly and fondly remembered as Field Marshal Sam Bahadur.

General Kaito's death shrouded over Naga Hills like an apparition; it was said that even the sky above the Hills, seemed to give an impression of stillness that day. At his native hometown Zunheboto, people plunged into total grief. His kith and kin were at their wits end; womenfolk in nearly all the Sümi villages shed their tears for the departed warrior; even the toughest soldiers' eyes were flooded with tears. Menfolk who had gone to their workplaces or to tend their fields, were totally detached from their work by the tragic news of their leader's death. Parents told their young ones, "Nagas have lost our greatest son." It was their bravest son who had been slain. Sümi tribesmen always held him in high regard. In the Sümi Naga realm, Kaito and Kughato were also looked upon as Chiefs of the Zhimomi clan. The Sümis were one of the few tribes to have the Chieftain System in their polity.

Alas! No amount of deeds could dare to bring back this mortal warrior from death! The hopes people had pinned upon this great fighter had been shattered; prospects were weaned away in no time. His existence was like an ephemeral star, brightest of all, but short-lived! Faithful followers and the workforce of Kaito's Army Government were blazing with rage to avenge the death of their leader. Craving for revenge within the followers had soared to its peak as the young leader was laid to rest. The after-effects of the assassination was massive; within days of Kaito's death, the authorities of his Army Government went about openly accusing the Phizo camp for the assassination. Meanwhile, at the Headquarters' of FGN, the fighters had put down the lid of their lair tighter than ever before. Along with despair, panic enveloped the Hills. Peace promulgators like Longri Ao, and functionaries of the peace camp, were wholly dismayed. How miserable were; their tireless endeavour to bring harmony within the Naga fold had come to all-time low. Nagas had their daggers drawn; ready to strike each other at the first sign of provocation; all heavily armed!

A façade of optimism for the exploited. A hurdle behind enemy failures and weakness. The one who manoeuvred adversities into hopes, and steered the course of the Naga freedom struggle from a colossal barrier to an incredible stance. Kaito gave up the whole of himself and pledged an allegiance to defend the free will of his people. A personality, dreaded and admired by the enemies, envied by the slanderers, and revered by the followers. He possessed an uncommon valour rarely found. His brief yet inspiring legacy has stood the test of time, and shall continue to exist till the crack of doom. If ever a dead man had won a battle, it was Kaito. General Kaito Sukhai will long go down in history as the literal icon of heroism. He was an inspiration to thousands of youths and Nagas in general. It is said, "a life lived for others is a life worthwhile;" indeed, his was selfless; he was larger than life.

To honour his contribution to his people and his feats against remarkable odds, the Sümi tribe annually observes the anniversary of Kaito's death on 4th August, as the Sümi Patriots' Day. As a tribute to this legend, General Kaito's statue, along with his brother Kughato's, is erected at Satakha, Zunheboto. This small town is the gateway to Sümi headquarters in the west, also located a few miles away from Kaito's birthplace, Ghukhuyi village.

Epilogue

What Kaito predicted before he breathed his last has all come true after his death. The air had gone rife with bitterness in the Hills, as the age-old kinship amid the Nagas was mired in great turmoil. The impact of Kaito's assassination was so severe that it jolted the entire Nagas to their wits end. For his tribesmen and his faithful followers, it was the heaviest and the saddest blow ever. They felt so lost, angry and frustrated that they started withdrawing support to the FGN. The Federal Government of Nagaland was no longer in a position to uphold the sails of unity among the Nagas. It began to tumble down like a house of cards, and thereafter, just about went defunct. It was apparent that a firm-rooted and deeply determined leader like Kaito, was the main crux that had been cementing the accord within the Nagas during this whole dark episode of schism and chaos. Thus, his death had unleashed the malady of factional bigotry, which then had run amok; it surged from different ends, and henceforth, killings among the brotherhoods were no longer uncommon.

Three months prior to Kaito's assassination, the FGN was divided over the core issue of changing the Parliamentary form of government into a Presidential form of government. It later turned out that the main reason for the change had no real meaning other than deposing the top Sümi leaders from the FGN, set up by the prejudiced hands. And so afterwards, in retaliation for the unsolicited change of the mode of government, and also as an act of vengeance for assassinating their finest general, many FGN leaders started seceding from the FGN and formed a new group known as the Revolutionary Government of Nagaland (RGN). To the utter dismay of Naga people, both the Federal Government of Nagaland and the Revolutionary Government were no longer in a fit state to bear the brunt of the struggle. There were no competent leaders to lead the pack, and they eventually gave in to the dominance of Indian troops. At that point of time they were left with two choices; either render unto Ceaser and stay at ease, or continue pursuing their birth-right against the prevailing odds. It was on November 11, 1975, some few NNC-FGN leaders, neither with the consent of the Naga people or their fellow members, signed the infamous accord known as Shillong Accord with the Indian union. Therefore, on January 31, 1980, in retribution to this act, three Federal Naga leaders; Isak Chishi Swu, Thuingaleng Muivah, and S.S Khaplang, denounced the NNC-FGN and launched the new group known as the National Socialist Council of Nagalim (NSCN), so as to continue the fight and free the Nagas from the forced Indian regime. Once again, Naga Hills became a battle pitch for insurgency and a dreaded site of carnage and hostility. The fight for their inherent rights still lingers to this day.

Indolence, prejudices for whatever it might be; there are partly researched books written by some authors, which generally speak unkindly of General Kaito. Yet, it's not surprising, because in a conflict between differing entities, there is always a difference of opinion and ideas. However, it is a known fact that in a conflict such as this, the first casualty would always be the truth, and Kaito became the victim for living the truth. Some claim that he had fallen into the pit of Indian money. In contrast, money to this young General, is worth dimes. When Kaito died, he did not even own a house to shelter his family, or a single plot of land to his name, nor a means to sustain or educate his orphaned children! It's sad but true that right after Kaito's death, all his children were sent to foster care.

The claim that Kaito created the RGN was a false conclusion, as the RGN was formed on November 10 1968, which was three months after his assassination. In fact, when the FGN started deposing all the top Sümi leaders from the Federal leadership, the meeting to form the Revolutionary Government of Nagaland had already taken place some months prior to General Kaito's assassination. On the other hand, Kaito was totally against the formation of the RGN, which would be similar to FGN; he was rather firmly set with the new plan of forming the Army Government. Some slanderers even allege that Kaito was responsible for Naga soldiers transferring into the Indian Border Security Force. This was also another false acerbic assertion as this absorption transpired in 1973, which was five years after the cold-blooded murder of General Kaito. On the contrary, even if he had been alive then, apart from opposing the absorption, he would in no way have supported the formation of the Revolutionary Government of Nagaland. In fact, the RGNs were also the ones who opposed Kaito's decision to form an Army Government. There were many reasons why Kaito had to form an Army Government and the prime among them was that Nagas under NNC-FGN were divided into a huge mess. He knew that an Army government alone could unite the people so as to expedite the Naga issues. This was why he stuck to his plan - it was in the interest of the Naga people.

In conclusion, with honest and sincerity; Kaito's brethren in no way seek the path of vengeance. Rather, their hope is that the bitterness surrounding the tragic assassination of their notable leader can be healed. If only the Naga people can work towards the vision of greater unity and achieve the dream he wished for, then his death will not be in vain.

No one is finally dead until the ripples he created die away from this world. We believe the sacrifices and contribution of General Kaito Sukhai towards the Naga political struggle shall be remembered, and his legacy shall stand the test of time. Kaito's participation undeniably brought the ripple effect to the Naga Freedom Movement. His visit to London had shed light on the 'Naga's unknown war' to the outside world, from which it had been kept hidden. His selfless role and daring contribution to the Naga cause is an example that most leaders would do well to follow. There's no wreath or dirge to accompany the World's Youngest General; however, this book is how we will remember him!

General Kaito's grave at his native hometown Zunheboto

Epitaph on Kaito's grave

'SUMI PATRIOTS DAY' ORGANISED BY SUMI KIPHIMI KUQHAKULU ON AUGUST 4, 2021 WAS OBSERVED AT SUMI PATRIOTS MONOLITH, ALAHUTO COLONY & OLD TOWN COLONY JUNCTION, ZUNHEBOTO

Sümi Kiphimi Kuqhakulu (Sümi Students Union) observing the 53rd anniversary of his death on 4th August 2021, at his hometown Zunheboto. 4th August was declared as "Sümi Patriot's Day" observed annually to remember all the Sümi Patriots who died for the Naga Freedom Struggle.

In fond memory of their contributions to the Naga National cause, their tribesmen erected the statues of General Kaito Sukhai and his brother Kughato Sukhai at their Native hometown Satakha, Zunheboto.

PRIMARY SOURCES OF INFORMATION

1) Firsthand account with General Kaito narrated by Late. Hopong P Yimchunger Ex Angh FGN.
2) Firsthand account with General Kaito and Diary of "My trip to East Pakistan with General Kaito" by Zhevishe Aye, former Lt. Col. Naga Army.
3) Firsthand account with General Kaito narrated by Dr. H.S Rotokha, former Angh FGN.
4) Documents provided and first-hand account with General Kaito Narrated by J.P Vikugha, former Lt. Col and Commander Signal Corps Naga army
5) Firsthand account with General Kaito narrated by his younger brother Vikuto Zhimomi, former President Nagaland GB Federation and present Chairman Joint Forum of Nagaland GBs (Naga Chiefs) Federation and Nagaland Dobashis Association
6) Firsthand account with General Kaito narrated by Dr. Huskha Yepthomi former Sümi Hoho President and former PSO (Personal Security Officer) to General Kaito.
7) Firsthand account of first Indo-Naga battle narrated by Vikuho Zhimomi first batch Naga Army and Personal Security Officer to General Kaito.
8) Firsthand account with General Kaito by Dr. Hokishe Yepthomi Advisor Nagaland tribal council and brother-in-law of General Kaito.
9) Firsthand account of Mrs. Vitoli Hoky former President Sümi Totimi Hoho (Sümi Women's Organization) and also youngest sister of General Kaito Sukhai.
10) Firsthand account with General Kaito by Ihezhe Zhimomi, former Minister Government of Nagaland.
11) Documents collections on Naga National Movement provided by Vikashe Murumi.
12) Narration by Lieut. Gen. Yambemo Patton's family.
13) Firsthand account with General Kaito by Kiyeshe Zhimomi ex Naga Army.
14) Firsthand account and "Diary of my trip to East Pakistan" by Toshiho Naga, former PSO (Personal Security Officer) General Kaito and Lt. Col. Naga Army.
15) Firsthand account with General Kaito by Tokhuvi Tuccu former Brigadier Naga Army.
16) Firsthand account of "The first Indo-Naga Battle" by Late Khezheto Awomi first batch Naga Army.

17) Firsthand account with General Kaito by Zhekheto Zhimomi, former Naga Army.
18) Firsthand account with General Kaito by I.K. Sema former Deputy Chief Minister, Government of Nagaland.
19) Firsthand account with General Kaito by Atoli Sema, General Kaito's wife.
20) Firsthand account with General Kaito by Late Nagaholi, General Kaito's eldest daughter.
21) Firsthand account narrated by Dr. Hatling Kuki.
22) Documents from Nagaland State Archive.

BOOKS AND JOURNAL REFERENCES

1) Hails and Blames by Scato Swu, 2013, Heritage Publication House Nagaland.
2) The night of the guerillas by Nirmal Nibedon, First Edition: Lancers Publishers, November 1978.
3) 50 years of first Indo-Naga battle Hoshepu – Golden Jubilee souvenir 2005.
4) Sümi Kumla Pasu (I) (Sümi's contribution part I) by General Zuheto Swu, 23-01-2006.
5) 50th Anniversary Battle of Satakha souvenir book 24th March 2006.
6) The legends of Naga Revolution by Dr. K. Kuhoi Zhimomi. 2012.
7) Politics and Militancy of Nagaland by Dr. K. Kuhoi Zhimomi, 2002, Deep and Deep Publication PVT. Lt New-Delhi.
8) Wounded Tiger, the papers of Khodao Yanthan by Dr. Abraham Lotha, 18 August 2017, Heritage Publication House Nagaland.
9) Sümino Naga ghoshika ghenguno mulakeu (Sümi's role in the Naga political struggle) by Dr. V. Hokuto Zhimomi. Printed and Published at Graphic Printers Dimapur, Nagaland.
10) The Naga Saga by Kaka D. Iralu 3rd Edition 2009, published by Kaka D. Iralu.
11) The beginning of Indo-Naga war (Khekiye-Hoshepu village) September 1955, Nagaland posts editorial by Ihezhe Zhimomi Ex. minister 34 A/C Aghunato.
12) Nagaland a journey to India's forgotten frontier. Faber and Faber, London 2011- by Johnathan Glancy
13) The Naga National Rights and Movement-Naga National Council, Kohima Nagaland.
14) Nagas The Unknown War. An account by Gavin Young, 1962.

15) The Pioneers, Nagaland Post Editorial, dated 11-24-2018 by Khekaho Zhimomi.
16) Dimapur Government College journal volume -4, "The battle of Hoshepu" 2017-18 by Vivi Swu.
17) Tribute to General Kaito Sukhai, Nagaland post editorial, dated 4th August 2019, by Khekaho Zhimomi.
18) Undying Spirit of Freedom-Autobiography of Retd. Gen. Mowu, June 17, 2020, Heritage Publication House Nagaland.
19) Sümi Naga Labour Corp 100 years Jubilee Souvenir, 2018 by WWI Sümi Naga Labour Corps Association.
20) Sümi Phuthekuwo eno axulhe (The History of Sümi Migration) Sümi Hoho Publication 2021.
21) The Naga oddessy by Mr. Visier Meyasetsu Sanyu, 2017, Speaking Tiger, Publishing Private Limited.
22) The Lost Mission by Pekingto Y Jimo, Maurice Wylie Media, Your Inspirational Publisher, 2020.
23) Zhevishe Aye "Ixu Ghile" (Autobiography) 2019 published by Bitoli Aye Kiba.
24) 33 years of Naga insurgency by Dr. M. Horam, 1987.
25) The Naga story (first armed struggle in India) by Harish Chandola 2012, Chicken neck publication.
26) Press clippings from "The Daily herald" (UK) September 1962.
27) Photo taken in 1919 by J.P. Mills. Copyright held by Estate of J.P. Mills.

Contact the Authors
Kkzhimomi123@gmail.com

INSPIRED TO WRITE A BOOK?
Contact
Maurice Wylie Media
Your Inspirational Publisher

Based in Northern Ireland (UK) and distributing around the world.
www.MauriceWylieMedia.com

www.ingramcontent.com/pod-product-compliance
Lightning Source LLC
Chambersburg PA
CBHW071613080526
44588CB00010B/1117